Praise for
Kiss Me Again

"Barbara Wilson asks the tough questions that get at the heart of lost intimacy. She shares openly from her own life, offering godly wisdom and practical help for those who want to rediscover the glorious oneness God offers for married couples."

—LINDA DILLOW AND LORRAINE PINTUS, authors of *Intimate Issues*

"I'm positive that every woman will relate in one way or another. God has given Barbara Wilson the ability to teach women how to find true healing and hope. Her powerful message frees wives to embrace intimacy in marriage as He intended. Husbands, encourage your wives to read *Kiss Me Again*—or even better, read it with her. You'll both be glad you did."

—GARY SMALLEY, author of *From Anger to Intimacy* and *The Language of Sex*

"Married women will do a huge favor to themselves and their husbands when they read *Kiss Me Again*. With compassion and insight, Barbara Wilson shows how to reignite the intimacy wives long for."

—DR. KEVIN LEMAN, author of *Sheet Music* and *Have a New Husband by Friday*

"Barbara Wilson has provided an incredibly helpful tool in this book for anyone who is looking for sexual healing from their past. *Kiss Me Again* is practical and grounded. Don't miss out on this powerful message."

—DRS. LES AND LESLIE PARROTT, founders of RealRelationships.com and authors of *Love Talk* and *Crazy Good Sex*

"*Kiss Me Again* is an exceptional guide to through the shadows and snares of a sexual past. For every couple who wonders why sex is so much less than it could be, this book can help you break free of old memories and a divided

heart. I loved the unblushing honesty of Barbara's writing and immensely practical help she's offering. This is a book whose time is now."
—PAULA RINEHART, author of *Strong Women, Soft Hearts* and *Sex and the Soul of a Woman*

"This book has radically changed the face of our women's ministry! It brings radical change to lives, marriages, friendships, and relationships with God."
—RACHEL JOHNSTON, pastor of women's ministry, Bayside Church, Granite Bay, California

"Since Mary has gone though the sexual healing study, I've seen the both of us come to a more intimate relationship with each other and with God."
—A HUSBAND

"This book not only changed my life, it brought me back into the arms of my husband and to God where I belong."
—A WIFE

"I am so excited about my life with my husband today! I cannot explain to you how wonderful it was to wake up and see myself in the mirror as a whole and complete woman without one glimpse of shame or remorse!"
—A WIFE

"My wife communicates better, she has brought us closer in our relationship, she denies me less for sex and even initiates, she is more confident about her sexuality."
—A HUSBAND

"My husband and I have an incredible marriage that includes good communication, trust, and love…and now, thanks to your book, one heck of a sex life."
—A WIFE

Kiss
Me
Again

Kiss Me Again

Restoring Lost Intimacy
in Marriage

Barbara Wilson

MULTNOMAH
BOOKS

KISS ME AGAIN
PUBLISHED BY MULTNOMAH BOOKS
12265 Oracle Boulevard, Suite 200
Colorado Springs, Colorado 80921

All Scripture quotations, unless otherwise indicated, are taken from the Holy Bible,
New International Version®. NIV®. Copyright © 1973, 1978, 1984 by International
Bible Society. Used by permission of Zondervan Publishing House. All rights
reserved. Scripture quotations marked (NKJV) are taken from the New King James
Version®. Copyright © 1982 by Thomas Nelson Inc. Used by permission. All rights
reserved.

Details in some anecdotes and stories have been changed to protect the identities of
the persons involved.

ISBN 978-1-60142-158-6
ISBN 978-1-60142-159-3 (electronic)

Copyright © 2009 by Barbara Wilson

Published in association with the literary agency of Janet Kobobel Grant, Books &
Such, 4788 Carissa Avenue, Santa Rosa, CA 95405.

Published in the United States by WaterBrook Multnomah, an imprint of the Crown
Publishing Group, a division of Random House Inc., New York.

MULTNOMAH and its mountain colophon are registered trademarks of Random
House Inc.

Library of Congress Cataloging-in-Publication Data
Wilson, Barbara (Barbara T.)
    Kiss me again : restoring lost intimacy in marriage / Barbara Wilson.—1st ed.
        p. cm.
    Includes bibliographical references.
    ISBN 978-1-60142-158-6—ISBN 978-1-60142-159-3 (electronic) 1. Lust—
Religious aspects—Christianity. 2. Sex—Religious aspects—Christianity. I. Title.
    BV4627.L8W553 2009
    248.8'44—dc22

                            2009011264

Printed in the United States of America
2009—First Edition

10 9 8 7 6 5 4 3 2 1

Most WaterBrook Multnomah books are available at special quantity discounts when
purchased in bulk by corporations, organizations, and special-interest groups. Custom
imprinting or excerpting can also be done to fit special needs. For information, please
e-mail SpecialMarkets@WaterBrookMultnomah.com or call 1-800-603-7051.

*This book is dedicated to every woman
who has trusted God to heal her past,
restore her present, and
reignite her future.
It's been an honor and joy
to have witnessed your journey.
An even greater privilege
to share your stories
in this book.*

Contents

Introduction

After I wrote *The Invisible Bond: How to Break from Your Sexual Past,* I began to hear from countless married women who identified with my story. Like me, they loved their husbands, wanted to stay married, but struggled with sex. They yearned for physical and emotional closeness with their mates yet shunned their intimate advances. They wished their sexual relationship could be more and were dismayed that it was not. They wanted to *want* to give themselves unreservedly to their husbands but could not.

Does this describe you? If so, you're not alone.

After spending the past several years speaking and writing on this topic and leading hundreds through sexual healing, I've come to believe that sex is a universal problem in marriages. Most couples—including Christians—have sex before marriage. The sexual revolution has affected us all, lowering our resistance to the pressure to initiate sex before marriage. Since the sexual revolution began, sexual promiscuity has increased with each generation. Now, forty-plus years later, we're reaping the consequences of our choices. The number of STDs has increased from just two prior to 1960 to more than twenty now.[1] The rates of divorce, out of wedlock pregnancy, abortion, and child abuse, as well as use of pornography, have all increased. And there's another unexpected and uncounted consequence of the sexual revolution and promiscuous sex—the emotional and physical dysfunction evident in marriages today.

But there's good news. No matter what is in your sexual past, God can heal your wounds and restore your marriage. God can heal the sexual issues you are struggling with in marriage. He can reignite your desire and deepen your emotional bond with your husband. He's done it for me and countless others, and He wants to do it for you.

For the last four years I've been leading women through sexual healing using a Bible study that I wrote to accompany *The Invisible Bond*. What I've learned from these women led me to write this book. I've discovered that sex from the past is negatively impacting many marriages today. When most wives say no to sex now, it's because they said yes before. But as these women have trusted God to break past sexual bonds, heal their wounds, and restore their marriages, He has been faithful. Healing sets us free from our pasts so we can rebond with our husbands, letting us say yes once again.

Husbands, You're Invited Too

While I have written this book for wives, if you are a husband, you can benefit from it too.

Your wife loves you and cares about your relationship. She wants to grow closer to you emotionally and physically. She desires that your marriage be the best it can be, but something is holding her back in the area of sex.

Perhaps you have felt hurt or frustrated by her disinterest in sex. That's understandable. Because she loves you, your wife longs to heal whatever is stealing her desire. That's why she is reading this book.

By engaging with her in this process, you'll help her feel safe and loved, which will help her to open up more fully with you. You'll demonstrate your love for her, and that you want to join her in achieving complete oneness, sexually and emotionally, in your marriage. In the process, you might discover that you need healing as well.

You can't fix your wife; only God can. But He will use you in this healing journey as you support, encourage, and walk alongside her. Healing will set her free. To love you more, to give herself to you more—without restraint emotionally and physically. And yes, that will result in better sex.

What's Ahead

The first part of this book will help you understand how sex from the past may be affecting you and your marriage. It will give you insight and information about the emotional and sexual distance you may be feeling, as well as why your desire for sex with your husband has diminished.

The second part is all about healing. I'll walk you through specific steps to

- heal the wounds you've accumulated from your past,
- address current sexual struggles in your marriage,
- replace the lies you've internalized with God's truth, and
- rebond with your husband to restore the emotional and physical intimacy in your marriage.

Each chapter contains practical exercises, tools, and questions to help you apply what you are learning. At the back of the book is a study guide that will take you through deeper healing with God.

God loves you. He wants you to live in freedom and to delight in your sexual relationship with your husband. Many others have already followed this path to transformed lives and marriages. My prayer is that you'll say yes to God and embark on this journey. With His truth, you'll be set free.

Saying No When You Want to Say Yes

I never imagined I'd be writing about sex. If someone had told me even a few years ago that I'd be writing, speaking, and leading a ministry on sexual healing, I'd have had a good laugh. You see, I didn't enjoy sex very much, even as a young wife. It ranked right up there with doing dishes and changing diapers.

I thought I was the only one who felt this way, and I never talked about it with anyone. After all, Eric and I were the perfect Christian couple with the ideal family. The kind others might envy. We practically lived at church, and we attended a small group with other couples our age, learning and praying together. We served in our church, our community, and our children's school. We were great parents, great friends, great Christians, and great partners.

My husband was faithful, a good provider, a wonderful father. He helped around the house, came home after work, and didn't squander our money at the casino or bars. He went to church with me, shopped with me, and cuddled in bed with me. He loved me, and I loved him.

So what was my problem?

I wanted more. Our marriage was okay, maybe even good, but it wasn't great. Certainly not what I'd dreamed it would be or hoped it could be. Sounds selfish, I know. Many women, particularly those who are single or in violent, loveless, or faithless marriages, might have little sympathy for me. Some might have a few words to say *to* me. And I'd probably agree. In the museum of marriage, ours looked perfect. But as the saying goes, looks can be deceiving. In our case they were.

The struggle started early, within the first year, and twenty years and four kids later, it wasn't any better. Naively, wishfully, we would slam the bedroom door on our struggle each morning, hoping it would stay out of sight. Out of mind. But with our glances and glares, with our barely there kisses, and with the words we did and didn't say, we erected an invisible wall of wounds between us. No one knew we had a problem. Not even us.

It was easy for me to overlook this segment of our relationship when everything else appeared to be okay. But what I didn't realize was that the wall I was raising in our physical intimacy was blocking our emotional intimacy as well. And although I tried, I couldn't keep this part of our marriage isolated from the rest. It seeped into every part of our relationship, stealing our joy.

We didn't fight often, but when we did, it was always about sex. The fights always started the same way.

"Why don't you like sex?" my husband would ask.

"I don't know," I'd respond. I wanted to like it, wanted to want it, but no matter how many times I promised to try, it never got better. I loved my husband, but I didn't love *making* love. So the fights usually ended up on my side of the bed. It was my problem, after all. I didn't like sex and avoided it with premeditated skill. When I couldn't evade it any longer, I was often unresponsive, longing for it to be over. If I never had sex again as long as I lived, I'd be *so* happy. And since my husband seemed to want sex all the time, I couldn't stand him much either at times.

I didn't understand why until God led us to fast from sex for a month. During that time Eric and I talked, especially about our struggles with sex. God began to show me how my past choices were limiting my ability to enjoy sex and feel emotionally close to my husband.

This revelation changed my life and put me on the road to healing.

DAMAGE FROM UNMARRIED SEX

You see, I lost my virginity when I was eighteen to the first boy I loved. I told myself it didn't matter because we planned to get married.

For the first ten months of our relationship, we made out a lot but didn't go all the way. As our emotional and physical intimacy grew, I began to trust him more. I felt I could depend on him to take care of me and put my well-being ahead of his own. After all, I wanted to spend my life with him, have children with him. I wanted him to be my protector and provider.

Then one day it happened. He might have planned it ahead; I don't know. We were alone in a park, and he decided that we'd been making out long enough. It was time to finish the deal. It took me by surprise, and somehow I couldn't say no. Plus, I loved him and trusted him. He wouldn't hurt me right?

Wrong.

It hurt. I didn't like it. I wanted him to stop.

Too late. He was finished. And I would never be the same.

I learned something about sex and men that day. It stayed with me, impacting my life and marriage until recently, when God healed my wounded heart. I internalized that sex is just for men's pleasure and that they'll use women to get sex. I decided that men don't care how we feel as long as they get what they want. He loved me—so I thought. And yet what he did didn't feel like love. *If this is how a man treats me when he loves me, then men cannot be trusted,* my heart whispered. *Especially when it comes to sex.*

Feeling humiliated, vulnerable, and used, I subconsciously erected a guard around my heart that day, telling myself that I would never let anyone hurt me again this way. At the time I denied my feelings because I loved him and we were getting married. We were young, and we eloped without my parents' blessing, unaware that the sex we'd had before marriage had sentenced our relationship to a rocky start.

When our marriage ended after two shaky years, my life began to crumble. By the time I was twenty-one, I had experienced marriage, divorce, promiscuity, pregnancy, and abortion. Not what I, a pastor's daughter, had envisioned for my life.

Then I met Eric. He was my do-over. My second chance. I determined that things would be different this time, but once again we had sex before marriage. But it was no big deal, I reasoned. After all, sex is just sex. Right? And getting married would clean the slate, make all the wrongs right. Right?

It sounded good. But it didn't work. The sexual experiences I'd had with my first husband and with men after my divorce caused me to associate sex with something unpleasant. Whenever Eric and I had sex, I couldn't shake the old feelings of being used, humiliated, and vulnerable. And the shame, condemnation, and regret I felt because I'd had premarital sex with Eric, and others before him, caused me to shut down emotionally and physically. Not only did the wall keep me *in,* it also kept him *out.* I'd brought these negative associations into our marriage and into our marriage bed. It inhibited my desire, enjoyment, and response to sex with my husband.

Can you relate? Is your marriage good, except for the sex?

As I speak on this topic, I hear similar stories over and over, all with this common thread: having sex before or outside marriage. Does that surprise you? With all the sexual pressures on us today, being a Christian doesn't guarantee virginity. It didn't for me, and I loved God and wanted to serve Him. A recent survey found that 95 percent of people will have sex before they get married, Christian or not.[1]

Of course, sex before marriage isn't the only cause of marital sexual struggles. You can have problems with sex even if you were a virgin on your wedding night. After all, sex is a complex, changing dynamic in marriage, and many things can contribute to its challenges. Male and female differences in sexual need and desire, outside pressures, hormones, pregnancy, unmet emotional needs, and parenting can all play a role in fluctuating desire and enjoyment of sex. Emotional and sexual intimacy will also be impaired if one or both spouses have been unfaithful or have an addiction, whether it be to pornography, alcohol, drugs, gambling, or something else.

However, after talking with numerous virgin and nonvirgin couples, I've discovered that the struggles for the nonvirgin greatly exceed that of the virgin. I often hear things like

- "Why was it a struggle to resist sex before I was married, but now that I am married, resisting it is all I do?"
- "Why could my husband turn me on before marriage, but now he turns me off?"
- "What happened to the great sex?"
- "What's happened to me?"

Can you relate to these women who love their husbands but don't enjoy sex? Your body is there, but your mind is elsewhere. Lying stiff and unresponsive, you long for it to end.

Whether your past is mild or traumatic, whether you've had multiple partners or one or two—and even if the only person you've had sex with is your spouse—sex from your past can haunt you in the present, impacting you and your marriage in a negative way. If in the past you had unmarried sex, in the present, *sex has you.*

JUST SEX? HARDLY

Sex is a big deal. Our culture has told us that it is just a physical act, that we can have sex and then move on without consequence to the next partner, repeating the cycle until we get married. However, sex doesn't work that way.

Arlene started having sex when she was twelve. Unbelievable, I know. Who knows anything about sex at that young age? She didn't, but the fifteen-year-old boy from her church youth group did. While luring her with romance, he stole her innocence and childhood with sex. For several years they carried on a secret sexual relationship, one she despised and enjoyed at the same time. She knew it was wrong, yet she felt trapped. Still, she felt special, loved, and desired by someone older and more experienced than she. Although the relationship ended, Arlene's sexual activity was just beginning. With her view of herself now wounded and twisted by this experience, she went on to experiment with alcohol and more sex throughout her teen and college years.

When she was in her thirties and married with two children, she came to me seeking help. "I want to love Sam with my whole heart, but it feels like I have a black rubber band around my heart, constricting me," she said. I knew exactly what she meant. The black rubber band was the sexual wounding she'd experienced, not only as a child of twelve, but also in her adolescent and college years. All that sex—all those partners.

No big deal, the world says. It's just sex. Hardly.

The lies about sex are rampant, and the worst lie is that sex before marriage won't ruin sex in marriage. Not true. Many of the sexual struggles in marriage today are a consequence of the sexual past of one or both of the partners. The damage brought about by unmarried sex is immeasurable—to our bodies, souls, and spirits.

Having learned as single women to guard our hearts from being hurt with sex, we can shut down emotionally and sexually in marriage. We may withdraw and become passive, or we may become dominant and controlling. Rather than feeling sexy, we clothe ourselves in shame, pain, regret. The power, the games, and the self-protection we learned in single sex become patterns in married sex. Purposely or inadvertently, we use sex as a means to manipulate, control, or exert our own way. To reward and punish. To show our love or to withhold it. Even if we were once the initiator, we now hold back, waiting for our husband to pursue, yet willing him not to.

God designed sex to unite the souls and bodies of two people. Sex outside God's plan affects us below the surface, in our souls and spirits. When we've created these sexual bonds outside marriage, we rob our partners and ourselves of the lifetime commitment our union was designed to seal. When we break up and move on, we leave behind parts of ourselves and bring with us parts of every partner we've ever had.

The wounds caused by these invisible soul bonds leave deep scars, which lead us to rely on destructive tactics to protect ourselves. They keep us guarded, untrusting, and closed off. If we don't trust our spouses, we may resent their desire for sex and lash out in anger. We may lose our desire for our spouses and fantasize about past lovers, or we may need pornography or alcohol to "get in the mood." We may even engage in addictive sexual behavior.

Yet seldom do we connect our present struggles with our sexual pasts. Instead we think: *There's something wrong with me. I married the wrong person. I should have married _____ [fill in the blank].*

Most of us don't seek help because we fail to recognize that yesterday's sex is revisiting us today. Marriage is not the giant eraser we wish it were—magically wiping all the past away. Saying "I do" at the altar doesn't erase all the times our body said "I do" in the past. Every time we have sex with someone, we're creating the "one flesh" bond God talks about in Genesis 2:24. Although we'd like to believe that the bond is cemented with "I do" in the presence of witnesses, the truth is that God created sex to be the "I do" that bonds us together for life. (I'll explain this in more detail in the next chapter.)

No wonder breakups involving sex are so painful, so wounding, so life changing. According to God and our bodies, every time we've had consensual sex with someone, we've married that person, and each breakup is a divorce. Breakups tear apart two who have literally become *one*. It's a hard reality to grasp, especially if we've had sex with many people. We try to minimize its impact, to declare it's no big deal. But our souls tell a different story: with each break up they absorb yet another blow as we limp on to our next pseudomarriage, repeating the cycle over and over.

A VIRGIN…OR NOT?

Some of you reading this may be thinking, *None of this applies to my situation because I was a virgin when I got married.* Many Christians have fallen for this deception—that sex only happens at intercourse, and that everything leading up to it is not sex.

That's what Beth thought. She convinced herself that she'd been a good girl by saving sex for marriage. But the only thing she'd saved was intercourse. Fifteen years later she was discovering how her sexual past was hurting her marriage. Although the news saddened her, she had hope—hope that through God's forgiveness and grace He could erase the past and heal the present.

For those of you proclaiming virginity on your wedding night, just how virgin were you? It's a seductive deception—this idea that sex only happens at intercourse. In reality, bonding occurs during sexual arousal and release, regardless of how it happens—intercourse or otherwise. Sadly, many of us were having sex long before our wedding night.

If this is you, let me say how sorry I am. But don't despair. I have good news.

GOOD NEWS

What God has done for me, He'll do for you. Not only can He break the invisible bonds you've created outside marriage, He can also heal the wounds they've caused.

Even the wounds you know nothing about.

Tell me, when was the last time you had sex with your husband? Honestly. For some it's been weeks, months, even years. For others it was just last night—but you were present in body only. Though you long for something more, you don't know how to get there. Until then, you're not looking forward to the next time or the one after that.

Do you find yourself exclaiming, "Finally, someone who feels like me"? Or, "Someone's finally asking the questions I've always been afraid to ask"? If so, I'm excited for you, because God has the answers to all your questions, including why you say no to sex now and how you can say yes again.

One of my favorite Bible verses is Joel 2:25, which says, "I will repay you for the years the locusts have eaten." In other words, God wants to pay us back, to restore to us all that's been stolen from us or destroyed. He's a master at taking the messes we make of our lives and turning them into messages of hope and healing. That's my story. It can be your story too. Just ask Arlene.

Arlene, whom you read about earlier, went through the sexual healing Bible study, and God healed her constricted, wounded heart. When asked to share what God has done in her life and marriage recently, she wrote:

> My feelings of guilt, shame, and regret are gone. My past is now just that, in the past. The sexual bonds I made outside my marriage are broken, and I feel bonded solely to Sam, the way God designed. That black rubber band around my heart has snapped, and I can now give my husband my whole heart.

I couldn't say it better. What God has done for Arlene, me, and countless others, He wants to do for you. I don't know what your story is or the extent of your marital strife. But God does. What you've come to accept as status quo in your marriage doesn't have to be. Although your secret struggles seem to have no end in sight, God tells you not to despair. He can restore you and your marriage to wholeness. He can take the mess of your life, your past, and turn it into a blessing, a message of hope and joy.

The "Superglue" Hormone

Okay, now it's time to talk about you. How do you feel about sex? I'm serious. Do you love it? just tolerate it? hate it? Maybe it's something you've never before thought about or put into words. But I'd like you to try. Take a moment and write down all the words this statement brings to mind.

Sex with my husband is_____

_____ [fill in the blank].

What came to mind? Did you write words like *wonderful, bonding, beautiful,* or *special*? Or did you write words like *nasty, dirty, unpleasant,* or *a chore*? Or maybe a little of both? If your response reflects the second list, you may be reluctant to admit it. I was, because it seemed that everyone around me—my husband, the media—told me I shouldn't feel the way I did about sex. Everyone else seemed to enjoy it. Why couldn't I? What was wrong with *me*?

I've discovered that many married women use negative terms to describe sex in the present. Yet they describe sex in the past, during their dating or partying days, as hot, steamy, passionate, and exciting. In fact, they couldn't seem to say no to sex. But now that they are married, they are struggling to say yes.

Jillian said that when she was single, the challenge of seducing men, many different men, fueled her desire for sex. "I didn't care about love; I just wanted to use men," she admitted. But now that she is no longer in pursuit of a sexual conquest and married to a husband she loves, her desire for sex has diminished. She's disappointed and confused.

Tina can relate. Before she married her husband, they had spontaneous and frequent sex. But the sex they'd had before marriage didn't follow them over the threshold. Once the initiator, Tina became passive, waiting for him to initiate, and he was waiting on her. With their feelings hurt and their expectations dashed, their sex life began to wane.

Why has sex become a problem for these couples? What happened? Why was sex so great before but boring and a chore now? Or worse, something to be avoided altogether? All good questions. And it may surprise you to find out that our brains hold the answer.[1]

CONDITIONED SEXUAL AROUSAL

What does the brain have to do with sex? It is our most important sex organ. As I pointed out in *The Invisible Bond*, everything that happens to us sexually begins in the brain, including arousal and the physiological response of sexual release. And like other organs in our body, the brain has chemical and hormonal functions. Two of the chemicals it releases are endorphins and enkephalins. These give us a sense of euphoria and well-being.

When we engage in activities that release these chemicals, such as aerobic activity, artistic or creative activities, intimate communication with a friend, and, of course, sex, the chemicals cause us to want to repeat the activity. But if we overuse one of the pathways to this chemical high, we can wander into addictive territory with that activity. This is why you see some people addicted to activities such as exercise, shopping, work, or sex.[2]

Unlike the other pathways, the sexual release pathway involves another component—sexual arousal. Sexual arousal prepares our bodies physiologically for sex. Dr. Douglas Weiss, an expert in the study of sexual addictions, says that we can train our brains to be sexually aroused by certain people, pictures, or thoughts because of our body's biological conditioning ability.[3] In other words, we can train our brains to be aroused by certain things or not be aroused by certain things.

Dr. Ivan Pavlov, a Russian physiologist, psychologist, and physician, first discovered our body's ability to be trained or conditioned to respond to certain stimuli. It started when he unexpectedly observed that the dogs in his lab responded differently to him when he was wearing his white lab coat from the way they did when he wasn't. He decided to do a formal experiment to study this unusual response. He began by first ringing a bell and then immediately feeding his dogs a treat. When the dogs ate, they'd salivate, which is a natural or involuntary response that helps with digestion. But what Pavlov observed was that within a short amount of time, the dogs began salivating as soon as they heard the bell ring, even without the presence of food. Pavlov called this a conditioned response. Dogs don't naturally salivate when they hear a bell ring. The bell had become a trigger, signaling the dog's brain that food was coming.

The same thing can happen to our brains with sex. Just as Pavlov conditioned the dogs to salivate when they heard the bell, we can condition our brains to respond to certain sexual triggers. Whatever we're looking at or focusing on during sexual release—a person, image, or thought—will over time trigger our brains to prepare for sexual pleasure and cause us to be aroused. If our husbands are the only one we've had sex with, then they will trigger sexual arousal in us. But if we have previously bonded to another person, or to an image or fantasy, then whatever we have bonded to in the past—and not our husband—will trigger arousal.

The combination of the chemical reward and the arousal trigger explains why the door to sex is difficult to close once we've opened it. Our body wants more sexual arousal and release, making it hard to stop. This is also why, when we break up and move on, we're more likely to have sex sooner in the next relationship. No wonder God tells us not to awaken or arouse sexual love before its time, in other words, before marriage (Song of Songs 2:7).

In order to understand this more fully, let's look at how these sexual bonds form and why they are so powerful.

THE HORMONE OF LOVE

Scientists have discovered that in addition to releasing chemicals during sex, the brain also releases a hormone called oxytocin, and these work together to create a strong bond between people. This invisible bond works like superglue, permanently attaching us emotionally and spiritually to a lover. This bonding happens with everyone with whom we have sex—whether we're married or single and whether the sex is consensual or forced. It's what God was talking about when He said that with sex "two will become one flesh" (Mark 10:8).

The past ten years have produced cutting-edge research on this hormone, which scientists have dubbed the hormone of love. Animal research has shown that oxytocin is involved in the nesting behavior of birds, cub-rearing in bears and lions, and the lifetime mating of prairie voles.[4] In humans, it plays a role in labor and delivery. But most recently, scientists have discovered its role in the bonding of human relationships. Produced by the body's pituitary gland, oxytocin is not only released into the blood during labor, delivery, and breast-feeding in women; it is also released in men and women during sexual arousal and release.

Some researchers believe that oxytocin is involved in the creation of deep feelings that become the foundation for love and trust. One researcher, Dr. Tom Insel, who is now director of the National Institute of Mental Health, examined two species that are practically identical genetically—the montane vole and the prairie vole.

He discovered that prairie voles stay for life with the partner they first copulate passionately with, and that, in contrast, the montane vole copulates randomly without forming partnerships. Suspecting oxytocin to be involved, he found that prairie voles produce significantly greater amounts of oxytocin than montane voles do. He also learned that when he blocked the oxytocin receptors in the prairie voles, they no longer formed partnerships during copulation. Dr. Insel is convinced that oxytocin is crucial to the development of long-term relationships, not just in voles but also in humans.[5]

Research indicates that oxytocin increases our ability to trust. When we trust, we relax, become vulnerable, and are able to give ourselves more freely to our spouses, especially during sex. Although research is still preliminary, it appears that the combination of chemicals, including oxytocin, that the brain releases during sexual arousal and release work together to create a strong bond between people. In *Hooked: New Science on How Casual Sex Is Affecting Our Children,* Doctors Joe McIlhaney and Freda McKissic Bush describe the chemical bonding of sex, saying, "Taken as a whole, these complicated processes [the release of chemicals including the hormone oxytocin] offer a compelling pattern. They are designed to lead toward and strengthen long-term monogamous relationships, supporting and reinforcing the family structure that is so vital to our survival."[6] Through sex we're bonded together spiritually, emotionally, and physically, laying a foundation of deep trust and affection for a lifetime partnership.

If we save sex for the one we spend our life with in marriage, then that person is the only one we bond to sexually. He is the only one who triggers sexual arousal for us, even years later when we do not look the same as when we were first attracted to each other. The more we have sex with that person, the stronger and stronger the bond becomes and the deeper our love for each other grows so that we increase our chances for lifetime commitment. When we save sex for the person we marry, not only is our arousal trigger exclusive to our marriage partner, but the release of oxytocin during sex strengthens and deepens our bond, ensuring our commitment to each other during the stress and difficulties that come with life and marriage. The chemical release and arousal trigger compels us to have sex over and over again, and the oxytocin ensures that we want to do it with the same person.

When Less Oxytocin Gets Released

But what happens when we don't save sex for marriage? Or when we've had sex with many people? Can these scenarios impact our ability to bond with our husbands? Unfortunately, yes.

Preliminary research has indicated that when we have sex and then break up, we release less oxytocin *with each new partner*. As we saw in chapter 1, marriage doesn't wipe previous relationships away. We bring each past partner into marriage, along with our impaired bonding hormone, hindering our ability to bond with our spouses. In one study, twenty-five women were asked to recall past relationships, whether negative or positive. Their oxytocin levels fell when they recalled a negative emotional relationship, and the levels rose when they remembered a positive relationship. The researchers conducting the study concluded that "previous relationship experiences can alter sexual bonding by altering the release of the biochemical 'superglue.' If the relationship history is sufficiently adverse, women will lose their ability to bond."[7]

In his presentation at the 2006 National Abstinence Clearinghouse Conference, Dr. Eric Keroack explained why. He said that when we're in chronic physical or emotional pain our brains release endorphins, a natural pain reliever, to ease the pain. Every time we break up with someone with whom we have had sex, we accumulate more emotional pain, which causes our body to release endorphins chronically (longer than seventy-two hours). The chronic release of endorphins reduces the production and release of oxytocin, which then diminishes our ability to form lifelong bonds.[8]

So what does this have to do with sexual desire for our husbands? *Everything.*

KEEPING THE "WOW" ALIVE

As a relationship matures the chemicals that give us the high during sex, such as endorphins and enkephalins, begin to subside. If a couple has bonded well through the release of oxytocin, sex continues to have the same "wow" effect, even though fewer chemicals are being released. Oxytocin keeps sexual attraction, desire for each other, alive in well-bonded couples.

This may explain why over time some people become unattractive to their spouses or feel that they've fallen *out* of love. Without the oxytocin to keep the "wow" of sex alive, people lose desire for sex with their current partner when the chemicals subside. People who begin to experience this sexual withdrawal will sometimes bring new activities into the sexual relationship to stimulate excitement, or they may move on to someone new. Eric Keroack and John Diggs explain why:

> People who have misused their sexual faculty and become bonded to multiple persons will diminish the power of oxytocin to maintain a permanent bond with an individual. Because, just as in heroin addiction, when the receptors become accustomed to a certain level of endorphins, in the absence of oxytocin, the person involved will experience "sex withdrawal" and will need to move on to a "new and more exciting" environment, that is, a new sex playmate.[9]

I believe the lack of oxytocin explains why married men and women are escaping into emotional and sexual affairs. These couples have never completely bonded. It's why married couples become bored with sex, and are no longer attracted to each other. They haven't developed that deep foundation of love and trust that keeps the sexual relationship alive and satisfying. Not surprisingly, studies show that couples who've been married the longest are the ones having the most frequent and satisfying sex. If they've bonded well, their love and trust has grown and their relationship has deepened and matured, making their emotional and sexual intimacy satisfying and fulfilling.

EVIDENCE SUPPORTS GOD'S PLAN

This research supports God's plan to save sex for marriage, as does the rise in the divorce rate. Prior to 1960, when most people saved sex for marriage, the divorce rate was 25 percent, but today, with most people having sex before marriage, the divorce rate has doubled. Research corroborates this correlation between premarital sex and divorce. A twenty-year study conducted by the University of Maryland and the National Center for Health Statistics, based on a representative sample of women ages fifteen to forty-four, found that "women who were sexually active prior to marriage faced a considerably higher risk of marital disruption than women who were virgin brides."[10] Andrew Greeley, professor of sociology at the University of Arizona and a research associate with the National Opinion Research Center (NORC) at the University of Chicago, confirmed these results in his study of premarital sex and marital infidelity. His research indicated that only 3 percent of spouses who did not engage in premarital sex with someone other than their present spouse were unfaithful in marriage. But of those who did have premarital sex, 12 percent were unfaithful in marriage. [11]

God is not trying to ruin our lives or spoil our fun by prohibiting sex outside marriage. He wants to protect us from forming bonds that can hinder our ability to have sexual and emotional intimacy in marriage. Even though age and hormones wither sexual drive, the bond that sex makes lasts a lifetime.

God's plan is perfect.

I was reminded of this not long ago while sitting across from a captivating couple at the airport. They had to be in their eighties, maybe early nineties, and wore their years gracefully, with dignity. Their abundance of wrinkles and shriveled stature didn't dampen the life exuding from them or the joy that warmed their faces. What captured my attention was how much they enjoyed each other. They were happy, snuggled together, holding hands. The whispering, giggling, and smiles displayed the intimate bond these two had forged throughout their decades together. They were a beautiful picture of sexual bonding the way God intended.

WHAT'S YOUR STORY?

But that's not how it happened for me. How about you? What if you, like me, had consensual sex before marriage? What if the sex you had before marriage was not consensual, but forced? What if you were raped or sexually abused? What if you saved sex for marriage but have used pornography for sexual release? Can these things impair your ability to bond with your spouse? The answer is yes.

But you have reason to hope. I want you to know that regardless of what's happened to you, God can heal you. He can heal your wounded emotions, your broken heart. Whatever has been robbed or destroyed in you, God can heal.

I don't know your story or the struggle you're currently having in your marriage. But God does. As you read the following true stories, pray and ask God to show you what bonding you've experienced in your past, and how past bonding is affecting your marriage today.

Sally's first sexual experience happened traumatically with date rape when she was sixteen. A year later she began dating a friend. He was a lot of fun, although definitely not the marrying kind. But she wasn't looking to get married—yet. So for the next several years, Sally enjoyed a wild ride of sex, drinking, and partying with him. Then she met her husband, a Christian and the perfect marrying kind of guy. Within a year they'd tied the knot. A decade and three kids later, Sally was bored and unfulfilled sexually, and she started fantasizing about her first boyfriend. She didn't want to; she tried to stop many times without success. She wanted to be free from her sexual past so she could be present with her husband. But the more she lingered in what had been, the more dissatisfied she felt in the here and now. Sally had moved on to a new partner, but the bonds that had formed when she was raped and through her sexual relationship with her boyfriend were impairing her ability to bond with her husband. Even though her first sexual encounter was forced on her, it still created a bond, one that involved trauma and negative associations with sex.

I recently received an e-mail from a woman who's saving sex for marriage with the man she's engaged to. She had heard me speak on this topic on the radio and was wondering if her childhood sexual abuse would impact her marriage. Since the abuse was against her will, she wanted to know if it had really created a bond that would hurt her marriage.

I told her that even though the abuse had been against her will and was not what God had wanted for her, she had an invisible negative bond with her abuser. She may not have realized it yet, but sex for her was associated with shame, pain, and abuse. Unless she broke the negative bond and found healing, sex with her husband would trigger all the emotions she had experienced during her abuse, causing her to retreat emotionally and physically from her husband.

Some women minimize the trauma of abuse and date rape, telling themselves it was no big deal. Or that others get through it and so can they. Or that they were partly to blame. One woman who had been abused by her father shared with me that part of her shame was that her body had responded sexually against her will during the abuse. She came to associate the pleasurable feelings of arousal with shame and disgust. Years later when she married, those associations followed her into the marriage bed. Unbeknown to her, the invisible bond with her abusive father was hindering her emotional and physical intimacy with her husband and killing her desire for sex.

Rape or abuse is a big deal. If this is your story, please understand it wasn't your fault. Even so, you will not "get over it" on your own. Until you have healing, sex with your husband will continue to trigger negative emotions, including shame, that will prevent you from being able to trust him and be vulnerable with him emotionally and physically. The lack of trust and emotional intimacy will diminish your enjoyment of and desire for sex.

The use of pornography for sexual release is a big deal as well. Mila was exposed to pornography as a young child. By the time she was a teenager, she was using pornographic images to help her get sexual release. Unaware that she'd conditioned her brain to respond to pornography as her arousal trigger, she entered marriage fully expecting that she could leave her secret habit behind. Not so. Although she loved her husband, she couldn't make love with him, couldn't get aroused, without thinking of the images from her earlier years. Her constant struggle plagued her with shame and despair.

I've talked with numerous women who were exposed to pornography as young girls and then went on to become addicted as adults.

Many who no longer view it are still plagued during sex by the images that aroused them. If this is you, I'm so sorry. Pornography is hard to avoid in our sexualized culture. Many of us were exposed to it early by a friend or sibling, or we stumbled upon an adult's stash. Then against our will the images became permanently implanted in our thoughts, associated with strong feelings of fear or arousal.

Although you may feel powerless in this area, God can heal you from your addiction to pornography and give you victory over these images that threaten to hijack your thoughts. God is healing Mila, breaking her bond to pornography and giving her hope. He is giving her victory over these images and allowing her to be fully present with her husband during sex. He can do the same for you.

REBONDING IS POSSIBLE

After hearing me talk about the conditioning of sexual triggers and about oxytocin, many people have asked me, "Can I retrain my brain so that my arousal trigger is my spouse?" or, "Can I get my oxytocin back?" I believe you can. Why? Because that's what God did for me. Not only did He break the bonds to my past lovers, heal my wounds, and replace the lies I'd believed with His truth, but He also performed the greatest miracle of all. He restored my bonding hormone. That's right. God healed me and made it possible for me to rebond sexually with my husband of twenty-three years. Sound impossible? Of course it does. It *is* impossible—for us. But not for God. Matthew 19:26 says, "With man this is impossible, but with God *all* things are possible" (emphasis added). God can heal anything. And the best part? Not only *can* He, but He wants to. And He will.

Believe me when I say you can fall in love with your husband again. You can desire to have sex with him again. You can open up your heart to him again. It happened to me, and I've witnessed it again and again in others. In fact, husbands often e-mail me or come up to me at church and thank me for their *new* wives, for making their marriages come alive again. I smile and tell these husbands how happy I am for them, but it's nothing I've done. God is the One who breaks the sexual bonds we've created in the past, and who heals us so we can rebond in the present.

If you'll let Him, I know He can do it for you.

When Sex Doesn't Bring Pleasure

I lived with shame for twenty-five years. It shaped who I was, how I saw myself compared to others. And I always came up short. It was the filter through which all my relationships were measured. It was the voice that frequently reminded me that others would reject me if they knew. Shame kept me isolated, alone in my secrets. Whenever I'd start to feel good about who I was, memories about things I'd done would steal my joy and self-worth.

Shame stole other things too. My ability to be real, open, and honest with others, even my husband. My ability to enjoy being me, to fully appreciate my gifts, what I had to offer others. My ability to feel worthy of love and friendship, even from God. But mainly, shame kept my focus inward.

Shame causes us to hide from others and even from ourselves. We assume that admitting our faults and failures to others will elicit the same disgust we feel toward ourselves. So we hide and become defensive, controlling, and perfectionistic. We try to impress others with who we wish we were, not who we really are. In the process, we wound others with our self-loathing tactics, erecting walls that keep those in closest proximity the furthest away.

Often when I felt shame, I asked for forgiveness—*again. I must not have been sincere enough last time, so God hasn't forgiven me yet,* I told myself, trying to explain why my shame remained. Again and again, I asked God to forgive me, but shame kept me from believing He had.

Have you ever felt that way? Like you must continue to ask God to forgive you because the last several times didn't work?

HELD HOSTAGE

I'm not sure how this lie deceived me for so long. Despite growing up in church and hearing the gospel all of my life, I'd missed the truth when I needed it most. What is the truth? That forgiveness is contingent on only one thing—confession. First John 1:9 says, "If we confess our sins, He is faithful and just to forgive us our sins and to cleanse us from all unrighteousness" (NKJV). Where did I get the idea that we must confess our sins repeatedly before God forgives us? I'm not sure, but this verse promises that forgiveness is immediate and complete, finished upon our first confession. That means that God forgave me the first time I asked Him for forgiveness.

But if God had forgiven me, why couldn't I feel it?

I'll never forget the life-changing moment when God showed me how my shame held me hostage. I'd been given a tremendous honor and responsibility: our senior pastor had called to see if I would consider serving on the leadership team for our church. In prayer I sensed God saying yes. So I agreed.

In a get-to-know-you game on my first retreat for pastors and board members, I came face to face with a sea of shame. Spouses had been invited to the retreat, and each couple was asked, How did you and your spouse meet? What did you do on your first date? What did you do on your first five dates? I wanted to die. I felt exposed as shame stabbed me over and over. I couldn't very well answer, "Eric and I were having sex by our fifth date." Not exactly the board member kind of answer they were looking for. The trauma of that moment has erased my memory of what I did say, but I know I made something up.

The next morning during my quiet time with God, shame's taunting voice said, "If they knew about your past, they wouldn't have asked you to be on the board." I sat before God, thinking that He must agree with that statement. That He saw me the way I saw myself—shameful, sinful, dirty. But God had a wonderful gift for me that morning. He showed me that He didn't see me that way at all. I saw the filth, the ugliness, but He saw me as unblemished, holy, and perfect. Not because I was, but because Christ was. Because of what Jesus did for me on the cross, dying for every sin I'd ever committed or would commit, God saw me through His Son, Jesus. Because of my faith in a sinless Savior, God saw me without sin.

Jesus took all of our sin *on Himself.* Because of what He did, when we receive His gift of forgiveness, God doesn't see our sin anymore. He sees a brand-new us: we are unblemished, holy, and righteous because of Jesus in us.

That was the beginning of something new for me. When I realized I was truly forgiven, I became willing to go through the process of healing so I could be free from the shame. I knew God was asking me to do this. He'd already shown me that no matter how hard I tried, on my own I couldn't put my past behind me. But He was about to show me how He could do it for me.

HEALING AND FORGIVENESS

God began teaching me the difference between forgiveness and healing. And why for sexual sin, as opposed to other sins, I needed both. I came to understand that forgiveness happens immediately, when we confess our sins. Healing, however, happens over time. Healing involves confessing our sins to others—the very thing I vehemently opposed doing. In James 5:16 God tells us, "Therefore confess your sins to each other and pray for each other so that you may be healed." I began to see that although God had forgiven me for the shameful things I'd done, the wounding and pain caused by my abortion and sexual past were keeping me from feeling His forgiveness.

The Bible says that sexual sin, unlike stealing or lying, is a sin we commit against our own bodies. First Corinthians 6:18 says, "Flee from sexual immorality. All other sins a man [or woman] commits are outside his [or her] body, but he [or she] who sins sexually sins against his [or her] own body." Although other sins can harm our bodies, sexual sin, whether from our own choices or others' choices forced on us, wounds us at all levels—body, soul, and spirit. God says that the bond of sex is a mystery. It happens not only physically but also spiritually and emotionally. So when we experience sex outside God's plan, we wound every part of us—to our deepest core. Although God forgives us the moment we ask, the wounds and lies we accumulate stay with us, keeping us from feeling His forgiveness. Forgiveness reconciles us to God, but healing reconciles us to *us* and then to others, allowing us to *feel* God's forgiveness.

And forgive ourselves.

Before I go on, I want to give you a chance to invite Jesus into your life, if you've never done so before. You can know the One who loved you before you were born and died on the cross so that you would know His love and spend eternity with Him. Take a moment right now to thank Him for dying for you and bearing all your sin so that you can know God and His love. Tell Him you want Him to take over your life, thank Him for forgiving every sin you've ever done or will do, and ask Him to fill your heart with His love. Walking with God takes faith; it means trusting that He exists and that He will reward those who seek Him. Walking with God is also an adventure, not only for now but also for eternity.

If you said yes to Jesus, let me be the first to welcome you into the family of God. As His child, you now possess His Holy Spirit to teach you everything about God—starting with His amazing gift of forgiveness and grace.

Now it's time to explore what's behind your own feelings of shame and resentment so that you, too, can experience God's forgiveness and healing.

WHAT'S BEHIND YOUR NEGATIVE FEELINGS?

Do you regret having sex outside marriage? I know I do. So do many others. In fact, most people share our feelings. According to the National Campaign to Prevent Teen Pregnancy, 55 percent of sexually active boys and 72 percent of sexually active girls under age twenty said they wished they'd waited to have sex.[1] I would venture to say that all of the married women I've counseled wish they'd waited for marriage to have sex. So then, why do we have sex outside marriage when we really don't want to?

I don't know what your first sexual experience was like, but if you are like many women I've met, you didn't have a choice when it came to having sex, especially the first time. Whether it was sexual abuse, early exposure to sex through pornography, or pressure to have sex as a teen by someone older, many of us didn't believe that "no" was an option. Was that the case for you? It was for Brandee.

Her first introduction to sex was at the age of fifteen. She came from an alcoholic family, so it's not surprising that she found herself at a party where older boys encouraged her to drink. And drink she did. So much that she doesn't remember much of what happened that evening. One of the older boys offered to drive Brandee home. Her parents were not at home, and that's where it happened. Her first encounter with sex. Unwanted sex. Forced sex. Rape. In Brandee's bedroom, on her bed, in an empty house. All alone.

In that moment, Brandee's innocence, her childhood, was taken from her. Sex had been paired with force rather than desire, with violence instead of love. Her first sexual experience was the opposite of what she had dreamed it would be and against everything God had planned it to be. The trauma didn't end that night. Brandee's negative associations with sex stayed with her, first propelling her on a destructive course of promiscuity, then into sexual and emotional dysfunction in her marriage, and finally into divorce.

Perhaps you have a similar story. Maybe you had your first sexual encounter when you were a young teen because someone forced himself on you. "I encouraged it," you claim, "so it's my fault. I should have known better." Or maybe the guy told you, "You were asking for it." Don't believe it. These are lies. No, you shouldn't have had so much to drink or made out with guys you barely knew. But poor judgment doesn't make the violence against you *your* fault. Putting yourself in dangerous situations puts you at risk, but it doesn't make you responsible. If someone forces you to have sex, it's called rape or sexual abuse.

Perhaps when you were a child someone older than you touched you in places you sensed shouldn't be touched. But you didn't know for sure. After all, it was someone you trusted: your father, stepfather, grandfather, uncle, brother, or family friend. And your abuser told you it was a special relationship—something for just the two of you to share—a secret. In some ways it made you feel good, but inside it made you feel bad. Most of all you felt confused. And scared. Someone stole your childhood and innocence from you—and warped your view of sex and yourself.

That's what happened to Marty. Her grandfather started abusing her when she was just six. The abuse continued until she was twelve. The day she finally told her mom what was going on, her mother turned around and walked out of the room without saying a word. Marty knew then that she was on her own. No one would protect her. No one cared—not really—and so she no longer cared for herself. That's when her promiscuity began.

Sadly, when others have used and abused us, we no longer consider ourselves worthy of anything better, and so many of us seek love in the one thing that makes us feel special—sex. One woman explained why she went on to become promiscuous after childhood abuse, saying, "I'd rather offer sex first than have someone take it from me by force. At least then I'm in control." Other women go the opposite way after their abuse. Their fear and disgust of sex and men cause them to shut down sexually in order to protect them from getting into sexually compromising relationships outside marriage. Some of these women become so distrustful or contemptuous of men that they never marry; some gravitate toward intimate female relationships rather than relationships with men. If they do marry, many times their only other sexual partner before marriage was their spouse. However, they may engage in emotional or physical affairs or become promiscuous while married or in between marriages. Shame makes them feel worthless, and they use sex to try to feel loved and valued.

Perhaps, as is the case for others of us, your first sexual experience wasn't forced. Maybe, like a young girl who told me about her first sexual experience, you gave your body willingly because you were in love. She loved her boyfriend and expected sex to be something loving, special, intimate. But it was none of these. Instead it was hurried, with little caressing and no enjoyment for her. Her dream that sex with someone she loved would be everything her heart imagined was snatched away at a tender age. With nothing to compare her experience with, she assumed that sex must not be as special as she had imagined and never would be. Sex was "no big deal," certainly not something to wait for. Even more tragic, she believed the lie that *she* was nothing special and not worth waiting for either. And with the lies came the shame that, although her heart longed for more, she was a fool for believing in the fairy tale that it could be so.

What's behind your negative feelings about sex? Having heard so many women's stories, I believe I know the heart of what you will say. You're not alone. The heartbreaking tales of pain and shame are endless. And regardless of the details, the effect is the same. Whether we had sex outside marriage because of our own choice or because of another's choice forced on us, we all experience shame. Hard to believe, I know. But it's true.

(Note: If you have experienced the trauma of sexual abuse or rape, talk to a professional counselor who specializes in the area of abuse. In many cases the deep level of wounding from the trauma of rape or abuse may require special therapy and counseling in addition to the steps of healing offered in this book.)

DIFFERENT DETAILS, SAME NEGATIVE EMOTIONS

Shame isn't the only negative sex-related emotion that a woman brings into her marriage. Think back to your most painful breakup of a relationship that involved sex. How did you feel afterward? Betrayed, depressed, angry, anxious, lonely, scared? These are just a few of the emotions women name when I ask that question. Now multiply those emotions by the number of sexual relationships you've had that have ended. You are bringing all those negative feelings about sex into your marriage. No wonder you don't enjoy it.

We may seem to heal from each relationship because we no longer feel pain, but the negative emotions accumulate and leave scars. And the scars increase our anxiety, fear, and distrust in subsequent relationships. When our trust in someone has been betrayed through rape, abuse, or a relationship breakup, the betrayal leaves us broken, wounded, and unable to trust. The combination of these emotions can cause us to harden or get tough in order to protect ourselves. As we move into a new relationship, the anxiety and fear of a repeat betrayal causes us to build a fortress around our hearts and emotions so that we won't be hurt again.

Although it would seem that this hurt would scare us from having sex in the next relationship, as we saw in the last chapter, the opposite is true because we've opened the reward pathway and know that sex is good. We've experienced the closeness and intimacy of sex and want to experience these feelings again. And the pain we're experiencing makes us seek pain-relieving activities, one of which is…sex. And so we repeat the same mistake, hoping that this time it will be different. But it isn't, and because it's not, we accumulate wound upon wound.

Studies show that teens who initiate sex early go on to have a greater number of sexual partners. The more partners, the less likely they'll have stable, committed relationships in their thirties.[2] Wounded teens become wounded adults. Most of the adults I walk through healing started having sex as teenagers. Yet they're still not over the shame, the sense of betrayal, the regret, the guilt, and the self-recrimination—even decades later. They struggle sexually, relationally, and emotionally. Why? Because they associate sex with the negative emotions they experienced in past sexual relationships and separations. And although they've moved on to a new partner, they bring all the old ones with them, emotionally, spiritually, and chemically.

So although you love your husband, sex with him can trigger all the painful emotions associated with yesterday's sex, causing anxiety, fear, and distrust. Robbing your desire for sex. Making you disgusted with sex, as though it's bad or dirty. Associating sex with the pain of being used and rejected, being loved and left. Causing you to shut down and close off, hardening your heart so you won't be hurt again.

THE DAMAGE FROM EMOTIONAL HARDENING

Gordon Neufeld and Gabor Maté wrote about the emotional hardening that happens when we've been wounded by sex. In *Hold On to Your Kids,* they wrote that the earlier this wounding occurs in one's life, the greater the impact into adulthood: "Repeated experiences of separation or rejection following the powerful attachments created by sex can create a vulnerability that is too much to bear. Such experiences induce emotional scarring and hardening."[3]

The emotional scarring can inhibit our ability to release oxytocin and to bond effectively with our husbands. How so? As I mentioned in chapter 2, preliminary research reveals that women with negative past relationships show lower blood levels of oxytocin. These lower oxytocin levels indicate that repeated relationship failures, along with the accumulation of negative emotions, can inhibit us from releasing oxytocin with our future husbands and thereby affect our ability to fully bond with them.

In addition to helping us form relational bonds, the release of oxytocin also reduces fear and anxiety by enhancing relaxation and calmness. It "lowers blood pressure and other stress-related responses and…increases positive social behaviors, such as friendliness and a desire to connect."[4] One study found that lowered levels of oxytocin increased anxiety behaviors in female mice.[5] I know, we're not mice, but scientists believe that a similar effect happens in humans. If so, accumulated negative emotions from the failures of past relationships involving sex increase our anxiety, fear, and distrust, which in turn can reduce our oxytocin release and inhibit our ability to bond in future relationships. Feeling emotionally and physically distant from our husbands lowers our desire for them—and for sex.

WHEN WE DON'T FEEL PROTECTED

Until now we've been talking about the problems that come when we've had multiple sexual partners, but what if the *only* person you had sex with before marriage is your present husband? Are there negative effects from that? After all, he's the only one you've bonded with.

It's possible I've answered some of your questions already. Do you see yourself in any of the stories I've told? Do you experience shame, fear, anxiety, or distrust in your marriage? Do you struggle with not wanting to have sex with your husband? How does your desire for sex now compare with how you felt before you got married?

Although I can't speak to your specific situation, I know that most of the women I've talked with who had premarital sex with their husbands brought shame and regret into their marriages. If you've experienced feelings of guilt or shame because of your sexual involvement, the bonding that occurred with your husband will be associated with those negative emotions, which may cause you to associate sex with something shameful, wrong, dirty. Although marriage provides a temporary relief from these emotions, because you feel good that you've made something wrong right, before long the self-condemnation can again attack, causing you to shut down emotionally and physically.

It may not happen right away, and you may not even realize this is the root cause of your struggles with sex. I didn't. However, slowly, gradually, as difficulties arise in the marriage that are not resolved through communication or sex, we can begin to resent our husbands. We are irritated about many things—they don't help around the house, they demand their own way, they leave the toilet seat up, and so on. But rather than dig out the root of our discontent, we focus on the present situation, assuming its resolution will melt our anger and resentment. After all, it's easier to point the finger, blaming our husbands for our marital mess, than it is to address our own past pain.

And then resentment sets in. We don't realize it, and we may even be afraid to say it out loud. But I've discovered resentment to be a common emotion among the women I've talked with who had sex with their husbands before marriage. *Even women who initiated sex with their virgin husbands-to-be.* It doesn't seem fair, but it does make sense. How so?

I believe that when we feel that our husbands didn't protect us before marriage, we eventually may come to resent them—even if we were the ones pushing to have sex. When a man gives in or pursues sex with us before marriage, we feel betrayed. He has failed to meet our core need to be protected.

This is so important. I believe that God charges men to be the protectors of women, to protect not only from violence but also from moral impurity. Not just inside marriage with their wives, but outside marriage as well. Men are charged to protect all women—their sisters, mothers, daughters, and friends. I believe that God created women to receive men's protection, that we need and long for men to protect us, care for us, and love us. When our fathers, brothers, male friends, or husbands protect us, we feel secure, safe. The honor and love we feel in this security frees us to become all God created us to be.

In Ephesians 5:25–27, God commands husbands to love their wives the same way Christ loves us, making us holy, pure, unblemished. Their love before and in marriage should protect us from harm. Before marriage men are to honor women and their bodies and protect their purity. Inside marriage, a husband is to continue to protect his wife's purity in and out of the bedroom. He is supposed to protect their sexual relationship by not exposing her to pornography or other perversions and by not expecting her to participate in activities that devalue her, exploit her, or wound her.

But, unfortunately, when sin came into the world, men fell down in this area. Many are no longer our protectors but our violators, our abusers, our predators through sexual abuse, promiscuity, and pornography. That was the case with Meredith's husband. Unbeknown to her he had been involved in pornography before they married. He didn't think it was a problem. After all, it wasn't hurting him or his future wife. He wasn't being unfaithful to her because he wasn't having sex. But he was having sex—with himself and the myriad female images imprinted in his brain. He had become bonded to pornographic images in association with arousal. Like many men and women, he assumed that once married he would no longer need the pornography to satisfy his sexual needs because he'd have his wife. She would be all he needed. But within months of marriage, he was bored with sex and began to introduce pornography and other riskier, more perverse activities into their sex life. Meredith hated it, felt degraded by it. And unprotected.

The idea of your husband being your protector may be hard for you to hear, especially if you strive for a sense of independence, even in your marriage. But keep in mind that sexual wounding from the past can awaken the need for self-protection as a survival tactic. If the thought of someone else being your protector awakens a spirit of independence or control, or brings fear or disgust to the surface for you, ask God to show you what is at the root of your reaction. Someone who won't allow herself to be vulnerable and protected will have a hard time trusting God.

Protection is synonymous with love for many women. When we're protected, we feel securely loved and valued. When we're not, we question our worth. If your husband was willing to have sex before marriage, you may have told yourself he didn't value you enough or love you enough to wait. He wasn't strong enough, man enough, to resist. If he wants to introduce pornography or sexual activities that make you uncomfortable, you may feel that you're not enough for him—not thin enough, not sexy enough, not enjoyable enough on your own. These nagging doubts, along with shame and regret, fuel uncertainty and resentment. Stuffed down over time, these emotions can one day surface as anger or emotional withdrawal and will diminish your enjoyment of sex.

HURTING LEADS TO HEALING

What emotions are surfacing in you as you read this? Most of us have spent a lifetime denying our feelings in order to cope with the choices we've made or the things that have happened to us. But unless we allow ourselves to feel the emotions we have stuffed inside us, we can't heal. If we allow ourselves to stay numb, we won't see what God sees; we won't address what we need to address for healing.

If you are going to the doctor for a pain in your back, you don't take medication before you go because you don't want to mask the pain. If you can't feel the pain, you won't be able to tell the doctor where it hurts, and he won't be able to assess the severity of your pain or prescribe treatment. It works the same way with our emotional and spiritual pain. If we won't allow ourselves to feel it, God can't direct us to focus on what needs healing.

This is often the hardest part of healing because feeling our pain makes us vulnerable to being hurt again, and we've been protecting ourselves from pain for as long as we can remember. The difference is that we can trust God to *never* hurt us. In fact, He knows all about our pain. He feels it as deeply as we do, and He wants to offer us the comfort we never experienced but so desperately need. That may be hard for you to believe, if trust is an issue for you. But when the Bible describes Jesus' life on earth, it reveals Him as One who bore our burdens, carried our diseases, felt our sorrow and pain. I've experienced Him doing that in my own life, and I've felt *His* pain for others when they share their stories with me and when I pray for them.

A dear friend recently experienced the shocking pain of having her husband leave her after thirty years of marriage. One day I called to check on her. I heard the sob in her voice as she tried to sound normal. While I talked with her, I felt her sadness but was able to keep my own emotions under control. But that changed when I began to pray. The moment I started, intense sadness and pain overwhelmed me. I immediately began to weep. Although I've never suffered this kind of betrayal, I somehow knew how my friend felt. I felt it too. Yet I knew I was weeping not because of my pain for her but because of God's pain for her. He was bearing her pain, letting her know how much He hurt for her.

And unlike humans who share our pain and *try* to comfort us, God succeeds at comforting us…if we let Him. He knows and loves us more than any human can, and He knows exactly what will comfort us. We can trust God with our pain. Because when you give it to Him, He promises to bear your pain, to offer you the perfect comfort for your pain. But even more, He will *heal* your pain.

The hardest part is surrendering to Him. But as Sophie can tell you, if you do surrender, what you have to gain soars high above the pain you're sure to lose.

A Story of Healing

Sophie's first exposure to sex was at the age of fourteen, when she was raped by an acquaintance at a party. It must have been her fault, she reasoned, because she shouldn't have gone in the first place, shouldn't have drunk so much, shouldn't have been so trusting. The rape changed how she viewed everything—herself, sex, men. Never wanting to feel used and vulnerable again, Sophie began to initiate sex so she could stay in control. Throughout her high school and college years, partying and sex were a big part of her life. Then she met her husband. But two years into her marriage, Sophie began partying again, as though she were single. For the next five years, unbeknown to her husband, she had several emotional and physical affairs.

By the time I met her, it had been eight years since her last affair. She described a life-changing moment when she sensed God inviting her to surrender herself to Him and to exchange her promiscuous lifestyle for a godly one. She gratefully accepted the invitation, because she was disgusted with herself and her choices. Even though she'd been faithful to her husband since then, the shame she bore kept her emotionally and physically distant from him. She seldom looked him in the eyes for fear he would know the truth. And she couldn't remember the last time they'd had sex.

She confided to me that until she'd read my first book, *The Invisible Bond*, she'd planned to go to her grave with the truth of her sexual past. But as she read, she sensed God saying that healing would only come for her and her marriage if she was willing to surrender her past to Him and be willing to share it with others, including her husband. This was something she couldn't imagine doing. But as her healing progressed, so did her willingness to obey God in this unusual request.

As she walked through the steps of healing offered in the second half of *The Invisible Bond*, I saw God change her heart toward her husband, change her attitude toward sex, and remove the shame she'd carried most of her life. When she had completed all the steps, she felt God say, "It's time, Sophie." She knew what He meant. It was time to tell her husband the truth. As she prayerfully prepared to share her infidelity with him, she asked that I and a male counselor, a friend of her husband's, be there with her.

It was hard—hard for her to confess and hard for him to hear. But God had been preparing Sophie's heart with the right words to say and her husband's heart with the ears to receive. Her husband spent the next six months grieving as they processed the truth together with a marriage counselor. They worked hard. It was painful at times, but they allowed the pain to draw them closer together rather than separate them. As their emotional intimacy grew, their sex life improved.

Recently I asked Sophie how she felt about sex now compared to before her healing. She blushed as she shared that her desire for her husband had never been so strong. And the sex had never been better. With the exuberance of fresh love, she described a brand-new marriage. One restored to love, passion, and intimacy. Gone were the shame, the secrecy, the walls. God had done something incredible, indescribable, miraculous in her. The shame she'd planned to go to her grave with is now a glorious testimony to the amazing power of God in her life. No longer afraid of the past, Sophie is now using her story to lead others on this same healing, marriage-restoring journey, with this same all-powerful, miracle-working God.

Emotionally Divided

Kerry went out with her first boyfriend for ten months before they had sex. She was seventeen. They broke up shortly after that, because he had started cheating on her. In her second relationship, the sex started sooner—after two months. Within two weeks of meeting the man who would become her husband, she was having sex with him. Kerry just married her second husband, with whom she also had sex before marriage.

Does this relationship pattern sound similar to yours? It does to me. Just like Kerry, I started having sex with my first boyfriend about ten months into the relationship. But with my husband, it was within the second week. I've always regretted it. Why was it so easy for me to have sex with someone I barely knew? Have you ever wondered that as well?

I know now that it was because of the reward of sex and the closeness the bond creates. But I didn't understand this at the time. My generation had sex because we were in love, or thought we were. Mostly we were experiencing the chemical high of attraction. And once that pathway had been opened, we initiated sex sooner in the next relationship that elicited the same chemical "love" feelings.

TODAY'S HOOKING-UP CULTURE

Sadly, today's youth make our sexual progression look innocent. In the hooking-up culture, high school and college students have sex with people they don't even know. Sex is random, with multiple partners, with little or no commitment. It's about personal pleasure, sexual conquest, and power plays but seldom about love.

In *Unhooked: How Young Women Pursue Sex, Delay Love and Lose at Both,* Laura Sessions Stepp wrote:

> Hooking up can consist entirely of one kiss, or it can involve fondling, oral sex, anal sex, intercourse or any combination of those things. It can happen only once with a partner, several times during a week or over many months. Partners may know each other well, only slightly or not at all, even after they have hooked up regularly.... It is frequently unplanned, though it need not be. It can mean the start of something, the end of something or the whole of something.... Feelings are discouraged, and both partners share an understanding that either of them can walk away at any time.[1]

Stepp goes on to describe a generation of women who want love but not right now. They want it later, after college, and after careers have been established. They want to avoid the time-consuming effort of having a relationship but not the fun and excitement of sex. While they believe that playing the field will help them eventually find their soul mate (most said they do want to marry one day), the opposite is happening. Though these young women are determined to stay unattached, their minds and hearts betray them, causing them to feel hurt, rejected, used. The result is a generation of women who feel distrustful of men and unimpressed with sex. Dr. Stepp wrote that *cynical, dishonest,* and *selfish* are some of the adjectives that the girls she interviewed used to describe how hooking up can make them feel about guys, including guys they're interested in. She quoted one college girl as saying, "Bad breakups are enough to harm your ability to trust, but hookups really leave people wary of others."[2]

But even more alarming is the impact the hooking-up scene has on these women's ability to build true emotional intimacy in a relationship. During her research Stepp interviewed a young college girl who said:

> These days holding hands in public has more significance than
> having sex. I was thinking about how easily people will go to
> bed with someone, but how freaked out they would be if they
> had to walk around sober holding that person's hand. Sex used
> to be something that was intimate, and now it can almost
> impede intimacy in the traditional romantic sense. I realized the
> other day how long it's been since I've had a boyfriend I would
> walk around holding hands with. I miss that life.[3]

Is this the victory of the sexual revolution? The crowning glory of our sexual freedom? That holding hands would feel more intimate, caring, and romantic than the precious gift of sex? That having sex would be of less worth, would offer less commitment, than holding hands? It seems that with each generation since the sixties, we have lost a little bit more...of ourselves, our dignity, our self-worth. We have lost the value

of sex, love, and each other. We have jeopardized our future relationships and marriage. Casual sex can ruin the kind of intimate, romantic sex God wants us to have in marriage. But even more important,
casual sex often robs us of emotional intimacy and the skills we need to
build a relationship founded on friendship.

A FALSE SENSE OF INTIMACY

Here's what I see happening more and more. People are having sex early
in a relationship—very early. The more they have sex, the closer they
feel to each other due to the release of powerful chemicals and hormones that attach them permanently to each other. They don't feel close
because they know each other well. They feel close because of the sex.
It's a false sense of intimacy.

Think back to a past relationship of yours that did not involve sex.
What did you talk about? What did you do together? When sex is
absent in a relationship before marriage, couples usually spend time
talking, enjoying fun activities together. But once the physical relationship escalates, much of a couple's time together involves sex.

Sierra, twenty-one and single, told me, "Before we started having
sex, our relationship was fun, romantic. We enjoyed long walks, candle-
light dinners, playing games, hanging out with friends." She went on to
say that as the physical intimacy progressed, they began to isolate themselves more, hanging out at her boyfriend's apartment, alone. When she
came to me for counseling six months later, she struggled to remember
the last time they'd been to a movie, had dinner out, or done anything
fun. "Most of the time," she said, "we watch a movie at his apartment
and have sex, and then I go home."

As Sierra was discovering, sex can create an artificial intimacy that causes us to feel more emotionally attached than we actually are. The bond of sex convinces us that we have a deep level of intimacy, but that intimacy doesn't really exist. This false intimacy makes the relationship appear solid, giving the promise of a lifetime marriage. But then we get married. It doesn't take long before we notice how little we really know each other. Then the lack of emotional intimacy keeps us from feeling close to our spouses and dampens our desire for sex.

It wasn't until I was being trained to teach sexual abstinence in high schools and colleges that I realized that premarital sex was the cause of the problems in my own marriage. I learned from the curriculum how we build emotional intimacy in relationships and how having sex outside marriage can inhibit that emotional growth. I'd been nagged by the feeling that something was missing in my marriage. Eric and I loved each other and enjoyed our marriage, but I was lonely. Many times during our past twenty-three years together, I'd sensed that we avoided talking about real issues, heart matters. Oh, we talked often—about the kids, money, friends, the weekend—but we seldom talked about our longings, fears, doubts, or dreams. I knew there was a part of me Eric didn't know and part of him that I didn't know. Maybe we were afraid to know these things about each other. Or maybe we didn't know what or how to ask each other.

My greatest fear was that I'd married the wrong person. Has that ever crossed your mind? Has this question cast doubt and fear on your relationship? It did on mine, sometimes making me feel trapped, desperate. Yes, I loved my husband. After all, I shared a life with him, had children with him. But he certainly wasn't my soul mate. That reality engulfed me with despair, regret, and loneliness. Alone in the darkness of the night, in the unseen places of my soul, I would wander around, unable to answer nagging questions. *Why are we in this place?*

How did we get here? How can we find our way out? Will it always be like this?

So when I heard how sex outside marriage impacts emotional growth, I immediately realized that was our problem. Eric and I didn't know each other well. Suddenly our struggles made sense. I understood why we couldn't share our deepest souls with each other, why our communication seemed to skim the surface of what we wanted to say. Why, when we did venture deeper, we didn't stay there long before scurrying back to safer topics. We had bypassed the hard work of getting to know each other through the gradual process that communication in a friendship allows. The time we should have spent talking and sharing our hearts we spent having sex. The sex made us feel closer than we really were, deceiving us into believing we knew each other intimately. We didn't. And twenty-three years later, although we knew each other better, our emotional connection still wasn't what it should have been. What I needed it to be. My soul, parched from loneliness and isolation, was my witness.

But with the truth comes hope. When I came to see that the lack of intimacy in our marriage—emotional and physical—had a direct cause, it brought me peace and encouragement. This was a truth I could hold on to. Although I still didn't know how to make it better, I knew that God wouldn't show me something He wasn't willing to restore in me.

THE LEVELS OF INTIMACY

Intimacy can be defined as "a warm friendship developed through a long association." Imagine one of your dearest girlfriends. How long did it take before you were able to trust her completely, to know her deeply?

Being able to trust someone to accept you unconditionally, regardless of your differences, takes time and an abundance of communication.

Roger Hillerstrom not only counsels many couples who suffer from the lack of emotional intimacy but also researches and writes on this topic, along with his daughter, Karlyn. In *The Intimacy Cover-Up*, he described intimacy as progressing through "five levels, or depths of vulnerability."[4] According to Hillerstrom, emotional intimacy deepens in proportion to the depth of each person's level of vulnerability. True intimacy develops when both parties progress together through the levels. For example, if the woman is sharing at the highest level while the man is sharing at level three, she may feel that they're closer than they are. In truth their intimacy is measured by the person with the lower level of vulnerability. Regardless of whether or not the relationship is romantic, we need to work through these five levels to get to know each other intimately. The highest level is where the deepest level of intimacy is achieved, where each person feels completely free to share without the threat of rejection or abandonment.

In the Hillerstroms' model of the five levels of vulnerability, communication at level one, which I call Safe Communication, comprises facts and information. This is the kind of interaction we have with people we don't know well. It's the chitchat we share with the clerk at the grocery store or a stranger at a party. Some examples of this kind of communication include "Lousy weather we're having," "This is great pizza," or "My team won last night."

It's safe communication because there are no feelings, opinions, or personal vulnerability involved, and there is no risk of rejection. We're merely speaking facts. People communicating at this level share minimal intimacy.

At level two, which I call Others' Opinions and Beliefs, we start sharing other people's thoughts, beliefs, and opinions. We are beginning to reveal more of ourselves by association. We say things like, "My mother always says…" or "One of my favorite authors said…" Such statements help us test the other person's reaction to what we're sharing without offering our own opinions. By not directly sharing our own perspectives and beliefs, we're able to remain safe from criticism or rejection. After all, we're not sharing our own opinion, and even if we do agree with it, we are not telling the other person how we feel.

We're more vulnerable at the next level, Personal Opinions and Beliefs. At this level we begin to share our own thoughts, beliefs, and opinions. But as we could in the previous level, if we begin to feel too vulnerable, we can say we have switched our opinions or changed our mind in order to avoid conflict or pain.

The fourth level, My Feelings and Experiences, is where we progress from thoughts and beliefs to feelings and experiences. At this level we talk about our joys, pain, and failures. Our mistakes in the past, our dreams, and our goals. What we like or don't like. What makes us *us*. We're much more vulnerable at this level than we were at the previous levels because we can't change how we feel or the details of our personal history. If we sense we may be rejected or criticized because of past or current experiences, all we can do is try to convince others that we're no longer impacted by our past. We're no longer *that* person. We're different now.

Level five, My Needs, Emotions, and Desires, is the highest level of intimacy in human relationships. At this level there is no escape. Needs, desires, and emotional reactions don't change overnight. We can't convince someone we don't really feel a certain way after we've reacted emotionally to something the person has said or done. We can't take it back.

Communicating at this level means we offer someone the most vulnerable part of ourselves. When we share things like "I'm hurt when you don't call," "I need to feel respected by you," or "I want to spend my life with you," we're sharing not only our hurts but our desires and needs as well.

If I am talking with you on this level and you reject me, I have no choice but to feel the pain. You can also use what I share against me later. You can tell others, or you can bring it up at another time in order to hurt me again. Because of the real vulnerability involved, this level of intimacy requires the greatest amount of trust. If we've been vulnerable at this level with someone and then been hurt by that person, we'll be hesitant in the next relationship to open up. We may take much longer to share at this level in the future.

WHEN COUPLES AT A LOWER LEVEL HAVE SEX...

As you look at the five levels of intimacy, I'm sure you'd agree that the fifth or highest level is the healthiest and safest one in which to be having sex. If you feel loved and safe with the person you're having sex with, you'll feel relaxed. You'll be able to give yourself completely to the other person, making the sex more enjoyable.

If you don't feel safe or loved, you can still carry on the business of having sex, but your feeling of vulnerability may be associated with anxiety, fear, distrust. It's hard to relax and enjoy yourself when you're feeling anxious. I've discovered that women have a hard time reaching this highest level of intimacy if they've been wounded by sex in their pasts. They come into marriage guarded, unable to be fully vulnerable emotionally and physically with their husbands.

What happens if we have sex with someone we're not at the highest level with? What if the relationship is at level one, two, or three? If we haven't established true friendship at the highest level, sex becomes the replacement for the levels we haven't reached. Since we aren't able to communicate our needs adequately, we fulfill them with sex. We communicate love with sex and resolve conflicts with sex.

I think something else is going on when couples who aren't married have sex. I believe premarital sex actually inhibits emotional growth in relationships. Here's why. Once we have consensual sex with someone, we *feel* close to that person, even if we're not. And once we feel attached to him because of sex, it will be harder to take risks with him. Why? Because we're not married yet, and we have much more to lose. Most likely, we're thinking that he is the one we're going to marry. At least our bodies feel married. And because we don't want to risk losing him, we'll be more hesitant to do or say anything that might jeopardize the relationship. We perform so he'll stay. The problem is that when we feel closer than we are to someone and are unable to take the risks necessary for emotional growth, we often remain at the level of intimacy we had reached when we started having sex.

What happens when couples in this situation marry? *We're meant for each other*, we think, because the sex has made us feel bonded, close, perfect for each other. But before long, we realize we don't know each other well at all. And after we've hurt each other enough, we'll learn not to venture beyond the safe level of communication. We shy away from the vulnerability and risk of true intimacy. As conflicts escalate, sex ceases to be as effective in resolving them, and we feel resentful. Roger Hillerstrom wrote, "Sexually active couples often use the sensation of intimacy to deny the existence of conflict.... The source of conflict often remains hidden, in fact, until unresolved tension develops into resentment.... As resentment builds, sexual intercourse no longer feels intimate."[5] Once that happens, we feel as though the love we once had has vanished. This can have several outcomes.

Many of us stay married, live amicably, but reside in separate boxes emotionally, paralyzed and unable to grow closer. To the outside world we look like a happy, healthy couple, but behind the front door we suffer. Often it surfaces in our sexual relationship, especially for women. We associate sex with emotional intimacy, and if that is missing, sex loses meaning for us, and we lose our desire. Some couples wound each other too much, shut down completely, and end the marriage. Others of us seek to have our emotional needs met through emotional and physical affairs.

No wonder the divorce rate is so high. We are creating bonds with multiple partners before marriage, thereby inhibiting our ability to release oxytocin and form lifetime bonds, even after marriage. On top of that, when we marry someone with whom we've had premarital sex (particularly if it is early in our relationship), our emotional intimacy does not continue to deepen, keeping us from building the foundation of true friendship that would sustain us through the difficulties sure to come. When you add to this our lack of the skills we need to begin growing closer emotionally, you can see why people think it is easier to end the marriage and start over. Unfortunately they end up doing it all over again, the same as before. With the same results.

Some of you may not relate because you've always been an open book with others and have no difficulty sharing at the highest level in any relationship. Even men you had premarital sex with. Of the two sexes, women are definitely the more relational one, eager and equipped for emotional intimacy. But our eagerness for emotional intimacy can get us into trouble in relationships. Let me explain.

Because we desire closeness, some women can jump through the levels quickly, sharing with the other person at the highest level within hours or days. But unless both people are sharing at the same level, they haven't achieved true intimacy.[6] The level of communication is unbalanced. The woman is sharing at the needs, emotions, and desires level, but the man is responding with facts or opinions from level two or three. Although she feels intimate, he is not responding with the same level of vulnerability. The intimacy she feels doesn't really exist.

This false sense of intimacy can encourage women to pursue sex before marriage. If a woman feels unsure about where the relationship stands or doubts the emotional closeness she feels, she may push the physical limits to confirm that he feels the same way about her as she does about him. Of course, she knows that a guy's willingness to have sex with her doesn't indicate his feelings of love for her. But deep down, she's hoping it does.

Unfortunately, she hasn't given him time to get to know her well enough to love her. By having sex too early, she's inhibited his opportunity to reach a higher level of intimacy with her. Just because a man struggles with the kind of emotional intimacy a woman is comfortable with, it doesn't mean he doesn't have the potential to relate at that level, given the chance. But when a woman gives in to sex too soon, she may be denying him the chance to be the kind of soul mate she longs for. Then she marries him. And at some point in the marriage, she may come to resent him because he doesn't share emotional intimacy with her. Yet that may not be his fault alone. As we've seen, entering into a sexual relationship may have frozen the imbalance in place, long before the emotional intimacy had a chance to flourish.

This was definitely the case with my husband and me.

AN UNEXPECTED PATH TO HEALING

Part of my resentment toward Eric was that he was so shallow—or so I thought. I couldn't get him to talk with me at a deeper level, and I always assumed it was his fault. I still remember the day I heard God whisper, "How can you offer advice to others that you're not willing to take yourself?" I knew exactly what He was talking about. Here I was teaching young people how to preserve a lifetime marriage by saving sex and sharing with them the advice Roger Hillerstrom gives his clients, but I had ignored it for myself. Hillerstrom instructs couples in premarital counseling to stop having sex so they can get to the highest level of intimacy before their marriage. With this advice, he's saved several couples from marrying the wrong person. He also advises struggling married couples who had sex before marriage to stop having sex for a time so that they can progress to the highest level of intimacy.[7]

Although my husband and I weren't sitting in Hillerstrom's office seeking help, we might have been. Instead, I was sitting in God's counseling chair, and He was advising me to stop having sex in our marriage for a time so we could grow in intimacy. Was it crazy? Absolutely. Hard to do? Much harder than I anticipated. But was it worth it? A resounding *yes*.

When I told my husband that, by not having sex for a few weeks, our sex life might improve, he was all for it. We committed to one month of sexual abstinence. During that time God began to heal me from the wounds of my sexual past and show me the lies and negative associations with sex that I'd brought into our marriage.

I also went through a process of breaking the spiritual, emotional, and physical bonds I'd created with my past partners. It was the most amazing experience. As God was setting me free from the shame, wounds, and bonds of my past, Eric and I grew closer emotionally. We talked a lot—about many things, but mostly my struggles with sex.

When we resumed our sexual relationship on our anniversary, we celebrated by redoing the candle ceremony from our wedding. Back in 1981 when we got married, it was popular to light two individual candles and then, as a couple, light a third one, leaving the two candles lit to signify that, although we were one, we were also individuals. As I went through healing, I realized that this ceremony symbolized what had happened in our relationship. Our struggle to become one had been inhibited by our pasts. I'd kept my candle lit. My past was still alive, hurting my marriage.

So this time we used our individually lit candles to light the middle one as we told God and each other that we were no longer two but one. And then we blew out our individual candles, symbolizing that our pasts no longer impacted our present. Song of Songs 2:11–13 describes what God was doing in our relationship, and we read it together:

> See! The winter is past;
>> the rains are over and gone.
> Flowers appear on the earth;
>> the season of singing has come,
>> the cooing of doves
>> is heard in our land.
> The fig tree forms its early fruit;
>> the blossoming vines spread their fragrance.
>> Arise, come, my darling;
>> my beautiful one, come with me.

That was five years ago. I'm still amazed by the changes in me, our marriage, and our sex life. Some were immediate; others have happened gradually. But right away I noticed that my attitude toward sex had changed. I no longer saw it as an unpleasant duty. It no longer made me feel vulnerable or used. The lies I'd believed no longer inhibited my ability to be responsive sexually to my husband. With our newfound emotional intimacy, my husband and I were able to share more openly about sex, and my trust in him grew. The shame, the regret, the bonding to past relationships—all were gone.

Not only did I see sex differently, but I also saw my husband in a new light. He was no longer the bad guy, someone wanting to use me for sex. Instead, he was someone who loved me and wanted to show his love through sex.

Did my desire for sex increase as well? As we'll discuss in chapter 12, sexual desire can be affected by many things: age, hormones, pregnancy, and so on. Because I had entered early menopause, my depleted desire also had a physiological component. So while I didn't have an immediate increase in desire, what I did notice was that I no longer resisted sex. Without the negative baggage tying me down, I was able to respond to my husband's touch and find greater enjoyment in sex. This made me a more willing participant, and in time my desire for him did increase.

Today I have more desire for my husband sexually than I've ever had since we got married—*ever*. I'm not saying I feel like having sex every night, because I don't. As love matures, sex becomes more about quality than quantity. But the new bond we've been creating since my healing has made sex with my husband a positive thing. Along with the physical bond, I'm also for the first time able to experience the emotional and spiritual bond that comes with sex. These changes have increased the frequency and our enjoyment of sex, and I now look forward to future interludes.

I'm not suggesting that every married couple must fast from sex to experience healing. On the contrary. For some, increasing sexual intimacy will contribute to their healing. Please pray and ask God how He wants you to proceed. If you feel God is leading you to a time of sexual abstinence, and your husband is in agreement, make it for a limited time only, with a set date to resume.

A GLIMPSE INTO THE FUTURE GOD WANTS FOR YOU

Would you like to enjoy lovemaking rather than endure it? Is this the desire of your heart? Are you ready to shed the shame and pain that keeps you from loving yourself, life, and your husband with abandon? Are you ready for things to be different? Would you like to let go of the heavy burden you've been carrying? To be done with the shame that haunts you, condemns you? Then you're in the right place. This is your time. Today could be the day you embark on a brand-new path that leads to a future of healing, wholeness, and freedom.

Not sure it's possible? Or that it's for you? Let me give you a glimpse of what's waiting for you. Here's how women who have experienced healing now describe how they feel about themselves and about sex with their husbands:

- "Joyful"
- "Hopeful"
- "Unashamed"
- "Liberated"
- "More connected to my husband and to God"

- "Free from past relationships"
- "Passionate"
- "Open to sex"
- "Humbled, happy, loved, worthy, empowered"

Hard to believe, isn't it? Although these women had been able to keep their pasts secret from everyone, when it came to their healing, they didn't want to. The transformation that had happened on the inside, in their thoughts, hearts, and attitudes, was now displayed on the outside for all to see. On their faces—once downcast, now beaming. In their body language—once stiff and self-protective, now relaxed, open, approachable. In their eyes—once hesitant and diverted, now sparkling, focused, confident. And most noticeably, in their voices and words. Their words, once sad and self-defeating, were now positive and hopeful, other-focused rather than self-focused.

But the most exciting change I saw was that these women began to dream again. When we're weighed down with shame and pain, we expend considerable effort trying to stay in control emotionally. We work hard to convince everyone around us that we're okay. We can become so absorbed in our own emotional pain that we're not aware of anyone else's pain. More often, we blame others for how we feel. Often, the dreams we once had seem impossible, hidden under our long list of regrets. Our past accuses and condemns us, convincing us that we're no longer worthy of being used by God. We had our chance, but now it's gone. So we give up hoping, asking, dreaming.

Stella, a divorced single mother, had rarely left home during the past ten years of her life. She'd been depressed for so long that she couldn't remember feeling any other way. Life had been difficult for her. Love had betrayed her, abused her, and abandoned her. When we met to discuss her joining the sexual-healing Bible study, she didn't know if she could be part of a group. She hadn't done that in a long time, and she was afraid to trust others. The first night of the study she walked out partway through the evening because being around people was so uncomfortable for her. But she returned and then came to every session. Stella went from being the most intimidated member to the group's most encouraging cheerleader.

I ran into her at church several weeks after the study ended. I hardly recognized her. She was a different person. She had confidence, enthusiasm, and joy. She was nothing like the sad, timid woman I'd first met. But even more amazing was what she told me. She'd called our pastor of community care to offer her services to women going through depression. "You did what?" I asked. I couldn't believe my ears. Just a few weeks earlier, she had barely enough courage to talk to me, and now she was offering to help others—complete strangers, no less. Only God can transform an isolated and depressed heart into one that wants to serve others. Before her healing, this dream of helping others, of using her gifts, had never been a thought, let alone a possibility. But today it was her reality.

Do you have a hard time imagining God using *you*? He wants to, and He will. He won't waste your experiences or your pain. He will use them to comfort others and give them hope. Rick Warren wrote in *The Purpose Driven Life*, "The very experiences that you have resented or regretted most in life—the ones you've wanted to hide and forget—are the experiences God wants to use to help others. They *are* your ministry!"[8]

I remember the morning I read this and heard God whisper, "Barb, let me have your past." *No way*, I thought. I sensed that would mean I would have to share my story. I was having a hard enough time thinking about it in secret, let alone talking about it in public. But as I sat with God, an overwhelming peace came over me, comforting me with an unexplained assurance that everything was going to be okay.

As I said yes to God that morning, anticipation accompanied the peace. I felt that He had something exciting planned for me, and I wanted it. I even told Him He could do whatever He wanted with my story. In that moment I knew that I could trust Him with my past, and more important, I could trust Him with my future. I didn't know where to start, but God did, and He directed me, one step at a time.

Turn the page, and I'll begin sharing those steps with you, so that you too can find healing. It's scary, I know. But I'm asking you to trust me. I've been where you are. And now I'm here. Believe me, it's a far better place to be.

Where Does It Hurt?

People often ask me, "Do I need to dredge up the past in order to experience healing?" I tell them yes. The first step toward healing is acknowledging where we came from and how we got here. Before we can move ahead, we need to look back. We need to recognize the sexual wounds we've accumulated and identify how they're shaping us today. Healing begins with being honest with ourselves about the impact of our past on our present.

Mark 4:22 says, "For whatever is hidden is meant to be disclosed, and whatever is concealed is meant to be brought out into the open." When we disclose what has been hidden, it loses its power over us. Sounds simple, but it can be the hardest step.

Her husband convinced her to meet me. She came, hesitant, skeptical. Her marriage was in trouble and coming to see me was a last resort. In the few years she and her husband had been together, he'd hurt her in many ways, especially sexually. His abusive past, along with his addiction to pornography, had warped his view of sex and women, and as a result he wounded and abused her. She was angry, blaming him for the state of their marriage and for how she felt. She'd agreed to come to me with the intention of setting him straight. So when I started asking about *her* past, she wasn't happy about it.

I wasn't surprised when she told me of her childhood abuse and teenage rape. I'd recognized the signs. She sat protecting herself, arms crossed tightly in front of her. She was defensive, closed off, and expressionless; her eyes were angry and fearful. I could see she was in a lot of pain. And now she was also angry at me. Her husband was the problem, so why was I focusing on her?

While they'd both experienced indescribable pain and brought their brokenness into their marriage, wounding each other over and over as a result, he was the one who was ready for help. She wasn't. She wanted to talk about *his* problems, but she was not open to looking at her own. She didn't consider herself a contributor to their marital distress. She hadn't realized that the abuse in her marriage had triggered memories of her past abuse, causing her to shut down emotionally. She had retreated behind a high, thick wall of protection, lashing out whenever she felt threatened. Her greatest complaint was that she was lonely. She was angry that her husband didn't engage with her emotionally. Yet when he tried, her defensiveness and hostility shut him down, causing him to retreat to his own corner for comfort.

She was okay with his being open, but was not okay with being open herself. She closed her ears to the truth that her past was a noose around her neck, keeping her from the emotional intimacy she craved. She wanted to move on to someone new. But unfortunately, as I explained to her, even if she found someone new, without healing, *she* would be the same. And then the new would become like the old, once again.

I've discovered that when we point the finger at someone else, blaming another for our problems, it's often because we don't want to look at what we are contributing to the problem. And when we pray and ask God to change someone else, He won't start with that other individual. He'll start with us, not because the other person is without fault or doesn't have any problems. Even so, God begins to show us our problems.

This is where many people quit, because the truth is more painful than they'd imagined. Sadly, their journey is over before it has even started. But if you're still with me, that's not you. You're one of the brave ones.

Are you ready to bring out into the open the things that have been hidden? Okay. Let's begin.

MAKING A LIFE MAP

God knows everything about us; He knows us better than we know ourselves. So before you begin, take a moment and thank God for this journey He's taking you on. Ask Him to give you a sense of anticipation for what He has in store for you. Then ask Him to show you what you need to see, to guide and direct you to the events and memories you need to recall. To open your mind to remember and your heart to understand. Ask that you'll see your life as He sees it.

You'll notice that the following chart, or life map, is divided into four squares. The top left square is labeled "Ages 0 to 12," the top right square is labeled "Ages 13 to 19, the bottom left square reads "Ages 20 to 30," and the last square reads "Ages 30 to the present."

What's this about? you're probably wondering. The chart represents your life so far, and the four squares represent four different age ranges. Zero to 12 are your elementary years, 13 to 19 your adolescent years,

My Life Map	
Ages 0 to 12	Ages 13 to 19
Ages 20 to 30	Ages 30 to the present

20 to 30 your young adult years, and 30 to the present your adult years. You'll only fill out the squares that apply to you.

As you fill in the life map, ask yourself the following questions and write your answers in the appropriate sections.

1. What brought you joy during this period of your life?
2. What brought you pain?
3. Did anything traumatic happen to you during this period? (If yes, tell what happened.)
4. What was going on sexually in your life during these years?
5. Where did you see God working during this time in your life?

You can write a little or a lot, whatever works for you. You can also use the life map as a guide and write your story in a separate journal, like the women in our study do. There's no right or wrong way to do this. The life map is designed to offer you direction as you reflect on the significant events, especially the sexual events, of your past.

When you've filled in all the life stages that apply to you, write your answers to the following questions in the space provided.

1. In which life stage were you first exposed to sex? By whom? Was your first exposure childhood sexual abuse? childhood sexual experimentation? date rape? pressure from someone older to have sex when you were a young teen?

_____

_____

_____

_____

_____

_____

_____

_____

2. When and by whom were you first exposed to pornography?

_____

_____

_____

_____

3. When and with whom did you begin having consensual sex?

_____

_____

_____

_____

4. What was the most traumatic event in your life? At what age did it happen? How did it change the direction of your life? How has it impacted your subsequent relationships?

_____

_____

_____

_____

_____

_____

_____

_____

5. What new thing has God shown you that you've never seen before?

_____

_____

_____

_____

_____

_____

_____

6. How have the events of your earlier years shaped the rest of your life? your choice of men to date or marry? your relationships? your marriage(s)?

_____

_____

_____

_____

_____

_____

_____

7. How have you seen God guide your life to this point?

_____

_____

_____

_____

_____

_____

_____

How're you doing? It's painful looking back, I know. You may be wondering what good it does to recall painful life events. I promise that what doesn't make sense now will, if you persevere. You can't give God a past that you haven't identified or acknowledged. Trust that He's having you remember everything you need to recall—nothing more, nothing less.

TAKING INVENTORY OF YOUR SYMPTOMS AND PROBLEMS

Let's keep going. Look at the items listed in the columns in the next chart. Check all that you have ever experienced in your life, and note whether you experienced it in the past or are currently experiencing it, using "P" for past and "C" for current. Be honest with yourself. This is your journey. Your healing. Denying your struggles keeps you stuck in your pain. Acknowledging them is the first step to breaking their hold on you.

Have you experienced any of the following? Check all that apply:

_____ Schizophrenia

_____ Anxiety/panic attacks

_____ Suicide attempts

_____ Physical abuse

_____ Imprisonment

_____ Abortion.
How many? _____

_____ Cutting or other
self-destructive behaviors

_____ A baby outside marriage

_____ Depression

_____ Sexual abuse

_____ Alcohol abuse

_____ Promiscuity

_____ Affairs: past/present

_____ Eating disorders
(anorexia, bulimia,
overeating)

In this next exercise, check all the symptoms and problems you're experiencing now.

_____ Lack of energy

_____ Cannot enjoy life

_____ Memory problems

_____ Anxiety

_____ Fatigue

_____ Difficulty making decisions

_____ Distractibility

_____ Sexual indiscretions

_____ Socially withdrawn

_____ Eating disorder

_____ Alcohol use

_____ Guilt feelings

___ Racing thoughts	___ Poor concentration
___ Mood swings	___ Racing heart
___ Sexual difficulties	___ Stomach problems
___ Physical numbness	___ Sleeping too much
___ Panic attacks	___ Apathy
___ Nightmares	___ Numbing out
___ Drug use	___ Distrust
___ Insomnia	___ Buying sprees
___ Disturbing memories	___ High-risk activities
___ Low self-esteem	___ Unsure of identity
___ Poor appetite	___ Frequent physical illness
___ Headaches	___ Hearing voices
___ Flashbacks	___ Losing track of time
___ Anger outbursts	___ Unsure of reality
___ Suicidal thoughts	___ Wishing to die
___ Reliving past events	___ Unwanted thoughts
___ No loving feelings	___ Weight change
___ Fears	___ Depression

Look over the items you've marked. This is you right now. These symptoms and problems offer a clear picture of how you're coping with whatever has or is impacting your life. It's easy to think that because the past is in the past, forgotten, it has nothing to do with who we are now. But if you marked any of the symptoms or problems in this exercise, it indicates that some of the emotional and behavioral symptoms you are experiencing in the present have a direct correlation to what has happened in your past.

When I filled out a similar form, I couldn't believe what a mess I was. I had no idea how much pain I felt until I saw it in black and white. I would have admitted that I could be better, but I would have said I was doing okay. Most of us experience symptoms we try to ignore or gloss over. They're something we sense or feel but can't explain or identify. But when we see in print words that describe what we haven't been able to articulate, we can no longer deny our true condition.

Now go back over the conditions and behaviors you checked and give each an intensity value from 1 for mild to 5 for extreme.

Next write down the three to five symptoms that trouble you the most.

1.

2.

3.

4.

5.

Beside each symptom, describe how long it has been troubling you. Your whole life? A few years? A few months?

WRITING WHAT YOU'RE DISCOVERING

Spend some time writing about all the new insights you're discovering— the good, the bad, the traumatic. Use these questions to guide your reflections.

1. How did earlier experiences determine your later choices and circumstances?

_____

_____

_____

_____

_____

2. Who else is to blame for things that have happened to you or
    the destructive paths you've walked?

_____

_____

_____

_____

_____

3. How have your past life events impacted who you are today?

_____

_____

_____

_____

_____

_____

_____

_____

_____

EVALUATING THE IMPACT OF YOUR PAST

Now that you've examined your past and identified some current behavioral symptoms, I want you to look at how your past has impacted your relationships, your view of yourself, your view of others, and your sexual relationship with your husband. Beside each statement below, respond with a rating from 0 to 3, with 0 signifying not currently experiencing, 1 for mild, 2 for moderate, and 3 for extreme. If a statement has more than one item or choice, please circle all that apply.[1]

____ I have difficulty expressing myself sexually.

____ I avoid times of sexual intimacy.

____ I avoid times of emotional intimacy.

____ I feel numb during sex.

____ I have feelings of grief/loss/sorrow/sadness.

____ I have feelings of regret/guilt/shame.

____ I am lonely, feel isolated, have difficulty making friends.

____ I feel "branded," as if other people can tell.

____ I feel different from other people.

____ I feel depressed/hopeless.

____ I have a general mistrust of men or women.

____ I have an inability to trust myself or my decisions (self-doubt).

____ I have feelings of anger/rage.

____ I have feelings of having been victimized.

____ I feel powerless to assert myself or protect myself against sexual harm.

____ I fear punishment.

____ I have dreams/nightmares/difficulty sleeping.

____ I have a fear of or discomfort with sex or with my sexuality.

____ I have seasons or cycles of depression/sickness/tending to be accident prone.

____ I experience flashbacks or hallucinations related to past experiences.

____ I have difficulty concentrating.

____ I have difficulty telling others about my past/tend to be secretive.

____ I have difficulty forgetting and/or remembering past sexual incidents.

____ I cry too easily/too much, or I'm unable to cry.

____ I feel "crazy."

____ I struggle with alcohol/drug addiction.

____ I need to use alcohol/drugs to engage in or enjoy sex.

____ I have suicidal thoughts/have made suicidal attempts.

____ I suffer from fatigue/tiredness.

____ I am having marital difficulties/marital stress.

____ I need to be in control.

____ I have been or currently am promiscuous (many sexual partners).

____ I feel unworthy of being loved or cared for.

____ I struggle with feelings/thoughts of lust.

____ I am sometimes tempted with sexual perversions.

____ I have self-punishing behaviors.

____ I struggle with desiring/enjoying sex with my spouse.

____ I need to fantasize or use pornography to be sexually aroused or to enjoy sex with my spouse.

____ I have no feeling of self-worth or feel inferior.

____ I struggle with self-condemnation or contempt for others.

You're doing great. Now look over your answers, and note those you marked with a 2 or 3. These are areas of struggle for you. You may be feeling discouraged right now, and that's normal for this stage. Although recognizing certain emotional and behavioral symptoms and feelings may be a new experience for you, you've had them for a while. Seeing them all at once, in black and white, can be overwhelming.

But they are no surprise to God. He knows you better than you know yourself. He's always seen what you never could. Yet He loves you anyway and wants to have a relationship with you, regardless. In fact, even if you don't go through healing, God could never love you any more or less. The greatest thing about God is that He loves us and wants us to come to Him just as we are right now…all messed up.

You don't need healing in order to become acceptable to God—you already are. Nor do you need healing so that He'll love you more. He already loves you more than you know or imagine. You need healing for yourself. So that you can remove the obstacles that keep you from feeling His love. Once you truly *know* God's love, you can freely share it with others. We can't give what we don't possess. Healing allows us to receive God's love so we can extend it to others. And receive love from them in return.

It hurts God to see you in so much pain. He's willing and ready to take all those 2s and 3s and turn them into 0s and 1s. If it's what you want, He's anxious to get started.

Okay, I have one more exercise that will help you disclose what has been hidden.

ACKNOWLEDGING YOUR CURRENT VIEW OF SEX

In chapter 2 I asked you what words come to mind when you think of sex. For this next exercise, I'd like you to write those words again. Write about the feelings that you associate with sex, how you would describe sex with your husband. Write about what sex is, and isn't for you—not about what you wish it was or what others say it is. Not about what you've read or heard sex should be, but how you feel about it right now. Don't spend too much time thinking about your answers; just write the first words that come to mind. Use present tense, as in "Sex is…"

_____

_____

_____

_____

_____

When we see in black and white how we feel about sex, it helps us acknowledge where we are at present and where we need to go. When you redo this exercise later in the book, you will have tangible proof of the healing God has done and will continue to do in you.

Assessing the Need for Housecleaning

Your story is unfolding. If your past includes early childhood sexual abuse, rape, pornography, promiscuity, premarital sex, affairs, or experimentation with homosexuality, you have negative associations about sex, and you've created a bond that's still with you today.

As we saw in the first part of this book, these bonds formed earlier in your life can hurt your marriage in ways you may not realize. And as you've seen from the inventory you took, wounds from your past can manifest themselves in the present through depression, insomnia, distrust, eating or cutting disorders, the use of alcohol or drugs to enjoy sex, or other behaviors. Some of these are more troublesome than others, but all impair our quality of life and can undermine intimacy in marriage. However, I want to highlight two behaviors—use of pornography and engaging in emotional or physical affairs—because the bonds they create wound you and your marriage and keep you from bonding with your spouse.

Pornography

If you used pornography in the past to become sexually aroused, then you might be struggling to become aroused during sex with your husband. Or you might be using it secretly for your own sexual release through self-stimulation. Or perhaps it is part of your sexual relationship in your current marriage.

If you or your husband has introduced pornography into your marriage, now is the time for some housecleaning. In Hebrews 13:4, God says to keep the marriage bed pure. When we bring other people into our marriage bed in our thoughts or with visual images, we involve them in our sexual relationship. And if we're imagining having sex with someone other than our spouse, we're committing adultery in our hearts, according to Matthew 5:27–28. God also warns us against sexual impurity, lustful passions, and obscenity, all of which are what pornography is all about.

If your husband is asking you to watch pornography during sex or is pressuring you to engage in activities that are humiliating or uncomfortable for you, talk with him about your concerns and how it makes you feel. You might say something like, "I want our sexual relationship to be the best it can be, but watching pornography, or engaging in this activity [name it] makes me feel humiliated, uncomfortable, degraded [use your own words here], and I'd like to stop."

Talk with him about the dangers of pornography. Not only do we become bonded to it, inhibiting our ability to bond to our spouses, but pornography also erodes emotional intimacy in marriage and devalues women, men, and sex. Pornography causes indescribable pain for wives who can never compete in looks or sexual prowess with the images capturing their husbands' attention. Women confess that the betrayal they feel when their husbands view pornography is as real as if they were having an affair. And the use of pornography can lead to perverse and degrading sexual acts, either in or outside the marriage.

If you feel that you need help in order to talk with your husband about this, ask him to go to a Christian counselor or trusted pastor with you. A wise third party may be able to help you express your concerns in a way that enables your husband to better understand your feelings.

Physical and Emotional Affairs

Some women who have experienced sexual wounding in their pasts seek relief for their pain in physical or emotional affairs. Their wounds keep them shut down emotionally and physically in their marriage, making them lonely and vulnerable to the advances of others.

If you're involved in a physical affair, I implore you to end it now. The Bible warns us in 1 Corinthians 6:18 to "flee from sexual immorality." Get as far away as you can, as fast as you can.

You may need help with ending the affair, especially if the person you're involved with is not supportive of dissolving the relationship. Pray and ask God who you should enlist to support and hold you accountable in this decision. In addition, eliminate any opportunities to see this person, and remove his contact information from your e-mail and phone. Although you may succeed in ending the physical relationship, realize that the bond you've created may prove stronger. You have an Enemy who will continue to tempt you to keep this relationship alive.

Most physical affairs begin as emotional affairs, which is why emotional affairs are so dangerous. Emotional affairs generally fit into one of two categories. One kind of emotional affair is similar in many ways to a marriage relationship, except the attraction is not expressed physically. But the emotional closeness, the familiarity, and the sharing of personal, intimate conversation can all lead to a sexual attraction and then to a physical affair. Plus, if you're fantasizing about having sex with this person or thinking of him during sexual release, you'll create a sexual bond with him over time. This may cause you to need to fantasize about him in order to be aroused during lovemaking with your husband. If you are involved in this kind of emotional affair, you need to end the close friendship you have with this person. If it's someone at church, remove yourself from opportunities to be with him. If it's someone you work with, seek and make the changes necessary to create distance between the two of you.

The other kind of emotional affair is one that a woman has in her mind, without the other person's knowledge. She imagines a closer, more intimate relationship than actually exists. This woman fantasizes about having sex with this person or imagines herself married to him. She dresses with him in mind, hoping that he'll notice her, or even better, that he will feel the same way about her. In fact, she'll misinterpret his glances, words, and gestures as proof that he feels the same way.

Both types of emotional affairs hurt marriages. They cause a woman to expend emotional energy on this person instead of on her husband. You should also realize that if you are fantasizing sexually about this person, God equates your fantasy with physical adultery (see Matthew 5:27–28). Ask Him to help you overcome these dangerous thoughts and turn your attention and emotional energy back to your husband.

We'll talk more about breaking these emotional bonds in chapter 7.

HEALING BEGINS IN BROKENNESS

I'm so sorry. I'm sorry for everything that's happened to you and every choice you or others made that has hurt you. But even more important, God is sorry. He knows and feels your pain. He weeps with you, for you. He longs for you to come to Him with your past, your pain, your shame. Isaiah 61:1–3 describes God's heart for you:

> He has sent me to bind up the brokenhearted,
>   to proclaim freedom for the captives
>   and release from darkness for the prisoners,
> to proclaim the year of the LORD's favor
>   and the day of vengeance of our God,
>   to comfort all who mourn,
> and provide for those who grieve in Zion—
>   to bestow on them a crown of beauty
>   instead of ashes,
>   the oil of gladness
>   instead of mourning,
>   and a garment of praise
>   instead of a spirit of despair.

If you're broken right now, feeling a deep sadness, that's good. God promises to heal your broken heart, to turn your sorrow into joy. He can take the mess of your life and turn it into a message of hope for others. Healing begins with a broken heart, but most of us don't like to feel deep sadness or pain. For many these feelings are a sign of weakness, so we try to be strong, unemotional, independent. Often when we're hurt, our hearts become hard, not broken. We may not realize that our hearts are hard. But God can't heal a hardened heart—only a broken one.

Ask God to show you if your heart has been hardened. It might be if you struggle with trusting God or others or if you are often negative and critical or blame others for your pain. If you've been as wounded as many of the women I meet, I understand why your heart is hard. It could even be justified. After all, who can you trust when most of those you trusted have hurt or betrayed you? God understands. He's not mad at you. He's not your accuser. And—unlike everyone else—He won't hurt you. You can trust Him with your heart. With your past. And with your future.

If you're tired of living in your mess, striving on your own to make it better, pretending that you're okay when you're not, give in to God. Not only does He want to bind up your broken heart and heal your wounds, but He also has a hopeful future planned for you. In Jeremiah 29:11 He says, "For I know the plans I have for you...plans to prosper you and not to harm you, plans to give you hope and a future."

If you're ready for the hope and future He has for you, I want you to pray the following prayer or your own version of it:

God, I give You my past. I want to be free from the shame and pain that haunts me today. I ask that You break my heart so You can heal it. I give You my present struggles, the things that have control over me. I ask You to set me free from addictions of my body and mind that are hurting me and my marriage. And I give You my future. I want the hope and future You have planned for me and my marriage. I surrender everything to You, every part of me, my past, present, and future. I ask that You forgive me, heal me, and set me free. I thank You in advance for all You're going to do to heal me and restore our marriage. In Jesus' name, amen.

You've just taken an important step. In fact, it's the most important step in this healing journey. You've said yes to God. And now He takes over. He is the One who has the power to change you. To set you free. You are powerless to do anything on your own, but God will do the work in you, so trust Him. Your part is to make yourself available to Him on this journey so He can do His work. Make time for Him. Listen to Him. Respond when He asks you to do something. Be honest with Him. Hold nothing back.

It takes a lot of courage to acknowledge your weaknesses, your need, your brokenness. Although I don't know you, I'm proud of you. God calls all of us, the whole world, to allow His light to shine into the dark places in our lives, but only a few say yes.

Now that you've identified your wounds, it's time to address them. Get ready. Because your eyes have not seen, nor have your ears ever heard, what God has prepared for those who say yes to Him.

6

A Plan for Healing

I don't want you to face your wounds alone. In fact, you can't "get over it" by yourself. That's the Enemy's tragic lie, and it keeps us stuck in a cycle of despair and destruction.

Not what you wanted to hear, I'm sure. Remember, God doesn't like secrets. James 5:16 reveals God's plan for healing: "Confess your sins to each other and pray for each other so that you may be healed." God uses others, especially the body of Christ, to help us heal. As I mentioned earlier, although forgiveness is immediate, healing from sexual wounds happens over time and with the support of others.

Don't worry. I'm not saying you have to go public with your past. You don't have to tell a lot of people your story. But you do need to include one or two others on your journey.

I know this can be scary, unthinkable. It was to me. Yet it was this step that began to dismantle the shame that was choking the life out of me. With each person I told, the telling got easier and my burden got lighter, allowing me to feel God's forgiveness. As Rick Warren has pointed out: "For God to use your painful experiences, you must be willing to share them. You have to stop covering them up, and you must honestly admit your faults, failures, and fears. Doing this will probably be your most effective ministry. People are always more encouraged when we share how God's grace helped us in weakness than when we brag about our strengths."[1]

My fear of condemnation kept me quiet, but when I began telling others my darkest secrets, I experienced grace. I thought people would reject me, judge me. Instead, they told me they could relate to me, to my story. Hurting people were drawn to me, sensing they could trust me with their pain. My new transparency became a magnet rather than a repellant. God wants to bring healing and restoration to those around us as well.

Starting with those closest to us, right at home.

ENLISTING THE SUPPORT OF YOUR HUSBAND

If you haven't already, consider inviting your husband to support you in this healing journey. God can use him to help you heal, and whether or not your husband has a sexual past, God may use this book to show him any past wounds that he's brought into your marriage unaware. Plus, the opportunity to communicate at this deeper level will enhance your emotional intimacy and foster a safe and loving environment in which you can completely heal.

Try saying this: "God has been showing me that the sexual struggles I'm having in our marriage are a result of things that happened in my past. I'm reading a book that explains how our sexual pasts can impact intimacy, and it offers steps to heal from our pasts so we can enjoy sexual and emotional intimacy in marriage. I love you and want to be able to share all of myself with you, sexually and otherwise, starting with this part of my life. I know that this healing journey is going to improve every part of our marriage, and it would mean so much to me if you'd be willing to walk it with me."

If your husband is not willing to join you, or if you're not ready to share your whole story with him yet, that's okay. Begin with yourself, and leave the rest up to God. He'll use your healing to reach your husband when the time is right. I promise. When we begin the healing process, others will often notice a change in us and want to know what caused it. Then, when we share with them what God is doing in us, we whet their appetite to discover healing for themselves.

If your husband does want to support you on this journey, tell him what you learned from the exercises in the previous chapter. Just one caution: many spouses don't want details—the dates and names of past lovers. It's just too hurtful. That's okay; the details are not necessary. Other spouses want to know everything. Or they may want to know it in stages. At first you might say, "God is showing me that I need healing from some things in my past, especially my sexual past. I would like to share it with you, but only if you want me to. Would you like to know about my past? If so, how much detail do you want?"

Then only share what he wants to know.

Your early conversations may be less specific, as in, "You're not my first." Then the conversation could progress to "I had six sexual partners before you." From there, if your spouse wants, you can give names, how old you were, how long you were in each relationship, whether the relationships were one-night stands, and so on. Don't overanalyze this step. There's no right or wrong way to do it. And if your husband doesn't want to know all the details, it doesn't mean you lack emotional closeness with him or that he doesn't love you enough to care. He's just not ready. Or perhaps he can't stand the thought of your being with other men or to have that mental image of you. Be willing to honor how he processes what you tell him. Your story is old news for you but brand-new for him. If you've had affairs in your past, or are currently involved in one, I'll address how to share that information with him in chapter 8. That part of your story needs to be addressed with sensitivity and wisdom.

One more thing: the above caution doesn't apply to childhood abuse or rape—violations against you. I encourage you to share those with your husband so that he understands that your lack of desire for him is not about him, but about the wounding you've suffered in your past.

ASKING A FRIEND TO WALK THIS JOURNEY WITH YOU

I also recommend that you ask a close female friend—a mentor, life coach, sister, mother, or Bible study leader—to walk this journey with you (even if your husband joins you). You need a friend to support you, pray with and for you and your marriage, and to help you process what God is showing you. You need a woman you can trust to hear your story and love you without judgment, someone who will be a confidante, who will help you decipher what God is saying to you. She can help you decide what and how to tell your husband.

Having a girlfriend to share with is important because as women, we understand each other. If you're like me, you have more words than your husband is able to absorb, so it's nice to have someone else to process with. Make sure your support person will keep what you share confidential and offer you grace, acceptance, and love rather than condemnation or judgment. This person needs to share your heart for God and to commit to praying for you.

Before you approach someone, pray and ask God to bring to mind the right person. When you're ready to ask that person, you might say something like, "God has shown me there are some things from my past I need healing from. The book I'm reading suggests having someone support me as I go through this healing. Someone who will meet with me, pray with and for me, and help me process what God is showing me. I prayed about whom to ask, and your name came to mind. Would you be willing to pray about being that person for me?"

At your first meeting, tell her what you've been learning and how it relates to you and your past. Tell her your story. Use your life map as a guide for telling your story, sharing whatever you feel God wants you to. You don't need to go into details—especially graphic details of abuse or rape. Doing so can leave unwanted mental images for you and the other person. Often the most shameful events, what you're most afraid to tell, are the things you need to tell; these are the things God is compelling you to share. You'll know what they are—your heart racing out of control will be your clue.

Give a copy of this book to your support person so she can read along with you. On my Web site, www.barbarawilson.org, you'll also find some guidelines that will help her support you on this journey. She'll need to know what you're learning in order to be an effective support person. And you never know: perhaps the courage you show in addressing your past will prompt her to do what she needs to do as well.

GETTING PROFESSIONAL HELP, IF NEEDED

In some cases, you may need yet another level of support—that of a professional counselor who can guide and support you in your healing.

If you're struggling with addiction to alcohol, drugs, sex, or pornography, I encourage you to enlist the help of a professional counselor. If you haven't gained victory over an addiction, the steps suggested in this book may bring to your mind memories and pain from your past that might trigger or escalate your addiction. I don't want that to happen to you. If you're aware of an addiction that you need help overcoming, find out if a church in your area offers a Celebrate Recovery program. Based on principles similar to those of Alcoholics Anonymous but with a Christian emphasis and suitable for all types of addictions, Celebrate Recovery offers weekly meetings, workbooks, and support groups for gender-specific addictions. Find out more about Celebrate Recovery, and learn if there's a group offered near you, at www.saddleback.com. If you don't have access to Celebrate Recovery, look for a local Alcoholics Anonymous or Sex Addicts Anonymous group.

If you've had early childhood sexual abuse or experienced the trauma of rape, be aware that this healing process may bring forgotten memories to the surface or trigger new ones. If so, you may need counseling from an expert in this area. Consider seeing a Christian counselor who's had training in Eye Movement Desensitization and Reprocessing (EMDR). It's an effective type of therapy for someone suffering from posttraumatic stress disorder caused by abuse, rape, or any other traumatic event. You can find out more about this therapy at the EMDR Institute Web site (www.emdr.com).

IDENTIFYING OTHERS WHO SHARE RESPONSIBILITY

When I was first asked to name those who shared responsibility for my pain, I could think of only one name. Mine. I alone was to blame for my choices, I assumed. As I was about to write my name across the circle in big letters, I was told I had to put other names down as well, that I could not write only my own.

How did she know what I was thinking? I wondered.

Obviously I wasn't alone in my thinking. Most of us, regardless of what happened in our past, assume responsibility for our pain, including those with past abuse and rape. But even if our pain was caused by our own choices, others had a part in those choices, in those circumstances. No matter what your sexual past, others contributed to what you've been exposed to. You didn't have sex by yourself; you didn't get pregnant alone or have an abortion alone. You were unaware pornography existed until someone else showed it to you or you innocently stumbled upon someone's secret stash. Whether it was parents who hurt you, neglected you, or weren't emotionally there for you or friends pressuring you to have sex or older siblings teaching or modeling promiscuous behavior—the circumstances of your past are not your responsibility alone. Who else had a part? It could have been a teacher, lover, society, or the Enemy scheming against you. It's time to face the truth. You've already known it deep down but have been afraid to think it or breathe it out loud for fear of the emotions that threaten to overwhelm you. I know. You're not the only one feeling this way.

Before you do this exercise, ask God to show you who else shares responsibility for the circumstances of your sexual past, whether that past includes abuse, rape, pornography, abortion, sexual promiscuity, homosexuality, or premarital sex with your husband. You also may want to include yourself. And even God. *Why didn't He protect me?* you may wonder. Don't worry, He can handle your anger. Whatever questions you have for Him, He's ready and willing to answer. Ask God to bring to mind the names of those responsible for sexual wounding in each of your life stages, and write them in the appropriate sections.

MY LIFE MAP	
Ages 0 to 12	Ages 13 to 19
Ages 20 to 30	Ages 30 to the present

GETTING IN TOUCH WITH YOUR ANGER

Are you feeling angry yet? It's okay if you are. If fact, it's a natural part of the healing journey. Once we acknowledge that others have played a part in our choices, we *should* be upset. Many of us have never admitted that we are angry; we don't even realize we feel this way. I didn't. But then I realized that all the anger I felt toward people in my past was being directed at those in my present life—my husband, children, parents, friends.

Anger turned inward often surfaces in physical and emotional illnesses, such as depression or chronic pain and fatigue. Don't be afraid of your feelings. Anger itself isn't bad. It's a God-given emotion. However, Ephesians 4:26–27 warns that anger is harmful when we use it to hurt others or allow it to take root. This exercise will help you direct your fury to the appropriate source and to express it in a healthy, helpful way.

Now that you've identified those who had a role in your painful past, I want you to write a letter to each person and express how what that person did has made you feel. "What?" I imagine you gasping. Don't worry: you're not going to give anyone the letter. This is about your redemption, not theirs. This exercise will help you get in touch with the anger and pain you've buried all these years, so that God can release you from the emotions. So that they no longer have the power to choke or poison you. At some point God may lead you to share your letters, especially if someone you wrote to is close to you now—a spouse, parent, or friend. But that is not the purpose of this exercise, nor should it be your ultimate goal. This is not a hate fest or an opportunity for revenge. That would be a misuse of anger, using it to hurt others as they've hurt you. Instead, this is a chance for you to be honest with yourself and God about how each person's participation or neglect in your circumstances has impacted your life.

"Why write it down?" you may be asking. Good question. Something happens when we write out our feelings. The mysterious flow from heart and head to pen allows for insight and understanding that don't result from thought alone. God uses the stark reality of black and white to show us truths we've never seen before. New feelings, thoughts, and memories reveal themselves. Take some time with this exercise. The emotions that will surface may overwhelm and drain you. You may be able to do only a few letters at a time. Once you have written all of them, read them to your support person or to your husband. Just as writing out your feelings and thoughts gives you added insight, reading your letter out loud allows you to express it with the appropriate emotion.

Don't underestimate the power of this exercise to free you. The women who go through my sexual healing Bible study often report that reading their letters to the group was the turning point in their healing. Reading your letters aloud enables you to acknowledge what others have done to you and how that's made you feel. Even more, it validates your pain. We usually undervalue ourselves, negate our anger and our pain. We've stuffed these emotions, memories, and feelings away for too long. So when others acknowledge what has happened to us and validate our pain and anger, it brings healing.

Like me, you may be afraid of anger. I assumed it was a sin, so I spent considerable energy shoving it below the surface. But it didn't work. Although on the outside I appeared calm and in control, beneath the surface and below my awareness, my anger brewed itself into a serious depression. I didn't understand that an important stage of grieving is acknowledging our anger, getting it out. And that this is part of the healing process. So don't rush this step. Ask God to walk you through this stage so that you can empty yourself of every last drop of anger.

In addition to journaling, you may want to plan some physical activities to help you vent your anger. Physical activity releases reward chemicals, giving you a sense of well-being and easing emotional pain. So when you feel like your emotions will overwhelm you, go for a brisk walk, ride a bike, or do some other activity you enjoy. Even better, if you don't exercise regularly already, initiate a regular exercise routine. The ongoing release of chemicals during physical exertion will contribute to your healing and emotional well-being. Plus there's the side benefit of losing weight, which makes us all feel better!

ALLOWING SADNESS, GRIEVING YOUR LOSSES

As anger subsides, you may begin experiencing grief: a feeling of regret or loss. This is normal, and it's good. Don't be afraid. Allowing ourselves to mourn what we've lost is healthy and necessary. Grieving has to come before the healing can take place. In *How People Grow,* Henry Cloud and John Townsend said that "Grief is the one pain that heals all others. It is the most important pain there is."[2] God agrees. He says, "Sorrow is better than laughter, because a sad face is good for the heart" (Ecclesiastes 7:3). Mourning helps us acknowledge our pain and what we've lost, allowing us to finally let it all go. (*Note: if you're on antidepressant medication, or have been prone to depression, see your doctor if you sense that your depression is resuming or escalating. You may also want to see a Christian counselor to help you go through this part of your healing.*)

This step in your healing journey involves feeling a deep sadness about the things you have lost. Jesus said, "The thief comes only to steal and kill and destroy; I have come that they may have life, and have it to the full" (John 10:10). We have an Enemy who is intent on destroying us, on setting us up to fail. From the beginning of time, he's been using sex to do that. We didn't start out seeking sex. We were looking for love. We've always been that way—in fact, we're born with this need. To be special to someone. To be treasured, loved, adored.

In their book, *Captivating: Unveiling the Mystery of a Woman's Soul,* John and Stasi Eldredge wrote that every little girl is born with a question that she longs for others to answer for her:

> "Am I lovely? Do you see me? Do you want to see me? Are you
> captivated by what you find in me?" We live haunted by that
> Question, yet unaware that it still needs an answer…. We do
> not first bring our heart's Question to God, and too often,
> before we can, we are given answers in a very painful way. We
> are wounded into believing horrid things about ourselves. And
> so every woman comes into the world set up for a terrible
> heartbreak.[3]

How was your question answered? Very early on you were asking it, even if you didn't know it then. In fact, you're still asking that question. If the first people in your life were unable to answer your question because of their own brokenness, you were compelled to take it to others. Most girls took the question to the boys. And although we're all grown up now, our question remains, and the source of our answer is often still the same.

"Am I beautiful?" we ask.

"Am I desirable?"

"Do you want to know me, love me, treasure me?"

For many of us, our question was answered with affirmation by loving, involved fathers. Mine was. He's in heaven now, but on earth my father was kind, gentle, and loving. I was his special girl, he loved me, and I knew it. That gave me the strength to say no to sex as a teenager. But then I grew up and fell in love and transferred my search for the answer to this vital question to my boyfriend, who became my first husband. It was after he wounded and rejected me that I felt lost, turning to others to validate me. Turning to sex for attention and love.

Before I started having sex outside marriage, I knew who I was, what I wanted, where I was headed. I was happy with life, with me. Once I started having sex, all of that became uncertain. My confidence was drowned in doubt, my joy quenched by regret and shame. I no longer walked with my head held high; gone were my dreams of serving God with my life. And the worst part? I was no longer happy just being me, the independent me, me without a guy. I, alone, no longer mattered. So I went from one man to the next, believing that their desire for me went beyond sex. Hoping desperately that they wanted me for *me*—the inside me, the real me.

But I never found the answer I sought. Some men used me for their pleasure; others I used for mine. Some even loved me—a little, I think. But there was never anyone who loved me apart from sex. The answer to my question was unspoken but clear. I was wanted, loved, and treasured for sex, but I still wondered if I could be wanted, loved, and treasured for *me*.

I don't know who answered your question or how it was answered. But I do know that many women have learned from others' words or actions that they don't matter, that they're not beautiful, that no one treasures them. Maybe they got these answers as children or later, as young women.

If these were the answers you received, I'm so sorry.

Because these answers are not true. The One who created you, who died for you, who wants to live forever with *you* calls you His treasured possession, the apple of His eye. You are beautiful, you are treasured, and you are loved.

But the thief has used sex outside marriage to destroy that beauty in you. To rob you of the true answer to your heart's greatest question. What has he stolen or robbed from you? Your dignity, joy, peace? How about your feeling of self-worth, your innocence, your childhood? Maybe he stole your dream of a loving marriage. Or the chance to have the kind of bond God designed for you, the bond you desired. Many women were robbed of their virginity through abuse or rape. And we've all been robbed of the true answer to our question, "Are we worthy of love?"

Grieving our losses is an important part of our healing. But rather than doing so, when we've lost a dream, desire, or expectation, we sometimes chastise ourselves for wanting it, as though we are being self-ish or extravagant. We assume that because it never came to be, we must not have deserved it in the first place. What a tragic lie that leaves us mourning in self-destructive, unhealthy ways the rest of our lives. Unable and unwilling to acknowledge that what we've lost matters. And because it does matter, we need to grieve our loss as one would the loss of someone or something dear.

Whatever you've lost matters. More importantly, *you* matter. It's time to stop denying your anger and sadness and your losses and start accepting God's gift of healing—the opportunity to grieve. What have you lost? What has the thief taken from you? Write your answers to the questions in the space provided.

1. What has the thief destroyed in you or robbed you of because of your sexual past?

_____

_____

_____

_____

_____

_____

2. What losses are you grieving because of your past?

_____

_____

_____

_____

_____

3. Of all that's been destroyed, lost, or robbed, what do you
   want God to restore in you?

_____

_____

_____

_____

_____

REPLACING LIES WITH TRUTH

As you grieve, God will begin to show you the lies you've come to believe about yourself because of what you've lost. When we are robbed of our virginity or innocence, we believe that we don't matter any more. When we've made choices we're ashamed of, we believe that we no longer deserve something good in our lives. Worse, we believe we deserve all the bad things that happen to us. Or that the consequences we experience are God's punishment. We think we're not lovable, not worthy of love. God will never forgive us, nor will He ever use us again. We're dispensable, discardable, insignificant. Our lives are ruined; there is no hope. We have no future.

Lies, lies...all lies. The truth is nothing can separate us from His love (see Romans 8:35–39). He forgives *all* our sins the moment we ask (see 1 John 1:9). God can redeem anything (see Psalm 103:1–5). He's already taken all our punishment on Himself at the cross. There is no punishment for us when we accept His gift of salvation and forgiveness (see Romans 8:1). He has great plans for our future (see Jeremiah 29:11), and we are His "treasured possession" (Deuteronomy 7:6), the apple of His eye (see Psalm 17:8).

Pray and ask God to show you the lies you've believed about yourself because of your past. Write your answers to the questions in the space provided.

1. What are some lies you believe about yourself because of your past?

_____

_____

_____

_____

_____

_____

2. What are some lies you believe about your present situation because of your past?

_____

_____

_____

_____

_____

3. What are some lies you believe about your future because of your past?

_____

_____

_____

_____

_____

4.   How do you believe God sees you because of your past?

_____

_____

_____

_____

_____

_____

In contrast to what you believe, how does God truly see you? Insert your name in the blanks as you reflect on the following verses for the answer:

"Therefore, _____ as [one of] God's chosen people, holy and dearly loved" (Colossians 3:12).

"How great is the love the Father has lavished on _____, that [I] should be called [a child] of God." (1 John 3:1).

"The LORD your God has chosen _____ [to be] his treasured possession" (Deuteronomy 7:6).

"Keep _____ as the apple of your eye; hide _____ in the shadow of your wings" (Psalm 17:8).

"Since _____ [is] precious and honored in my

sight, and because I love _____.… Do not be
afraid, for I am with _____" (Isaiah 43:4–5).

"But now, this is what the LORD says—he who created you,
_____, he who formed you, _____:
'Fear not, for I have redeemed you; I have summoned you by
name; you are mine'" (Isaiah 43:1).

"I have engraved _____ on the palms of my
hands" (Isaiah 49:16).

It's time to stop believing the lies the Enemy's been feeding you—
lies that you're dirty, ugly, unworthy, unloved. Instead, take your question, your longings, your needs to God. He's the only One who can give
you the answer you long for…the only answer that's true.

"Am I beautiful?"

"Yes," He assures.

"Am I desirable?"

"Without question," He smiles.

"Do You want to know me, love me, treasure me?"

"Yes, *yes*, YES," He shouts for all to hear.

Can you hear Him?

Because He's talking to *you*.

Say Good-Bye to the Past

Lily recognized him right away. He was her first love. He lived in her old hometown, where she was visiting family. She came back every year, and every year she hoped she'd see him. Every time she saw him, little butterflies tickled her insides, transporting her back to their love-filled days. She hoped he'd notice her, still be attracted to her, as she was to him. No, she didn't have thoughts of leaving husband number two for him. But she loved seeing him, still felt attached to him, attracted to him. And she loved to tease him flirtatiously, leaving him no doubt as to what he'd missed out on, had let slip away.

Lily's experience is not uncommon. Until the bond is broken, we can, years later, still feel attached to earlier lovers, even though we've moved on. We may not think of them for long periods of time, but then something reminds us—a dream, an e-mail, a song, a comment— and they're instantly in our thoughts again. If we dwell on those thoughts, we can reignite old feelings and desires. If we're struggling in our marriages, feeling unloved or insecure, memories of past lovers can make us pine for what might have been. *Should I have married him*? we wonder. Some may move from thought to action by looking up old flames and initiating contact. That's what Lily was doing. Although she had no desire to dissolve her marriage, she loved to fantasize about her first love and what might have been.

When we think back to old relationships, we often remember only the positive, even if the relationship was difficult. Why? Because of the presence of oxytocin when the bond was created. According to Dr. Keroack, oxytocin has been found to improve the ability to recall positive events and to reduce the ability to recall negative events.[1] This helps explain why women will go through childbirth multiple times. And why some women return to abusive men. As they recall the fleeting happy moments in their relationships, they remain hopeful that things will get better.

But when Lily returned to her hometown after going through healing, something had changed. She felt no butterflies. No feeling of attachment. No desire to make her old love jealous, or regretful for having let her go. What made this time different from all the times before? Lily had allowed God to break the sexual bonds she'd created with all her past lovers—including this one—and to heal her wounds. What exactly did she do that severed this bond with him? I don't know for sure. What God accomplished in her is a mystery. None of the steps I'm asking you to do have any power in themselves. God is the One who does the work—by breaking the attachments, healing the hurts, replacing what we've lost. But I do know that He's been pleased to use the steps offered in this book as a means through which He does His work. Especially this next step.

Asking God to Break Sexual Bonds

As you recalled your life story, many sexual partners may have come to mind. Now I want you to ask God to show you *everyone* that you've created a sexual bond with.

I don't know who God will bring to your mind. I've provided a representative list of people and situations He may reveal. Your list may include some or all of these, or you may have some that aren't mentioned here. Don't worry. God knows what and who you need to break a bond with—and He may bring to mind some you wouldn't have thought necessary. Don't try to analyze whether something or someone should be on your list. Trust that whatever He brings to mind needs to be there. Your list may expand as the days and weeks go by. If God continues to bring more people to mind, make sure to add them.

Your list may include:

- Everyone you've had consensual sex with outside marriage— including those with whom you had long-term relationships, one-night stands, or physical affairs.
- Those with whom you've done everything but intercourse that included sexual arousal or release—oral sex, petting, mutual masturbation, and so on.
- Sexually stimulating material that you've experienced sexual arousal or release with—pornographic images in magazines, TV, the Internet, even steamy romance novels.
- Those who have sexually abused you, forced sex on you, raped you. (If you don't know the name of the person, that's okay.)
- Those of the same and/or opposite sex you have experimented sexually with—even as young children. (I'm talking not about

innocent childhood exploration, but about activities that are more deliberately sexual in nature. However, if God brings it to mind, put it on your list.)

• Your husband, if you had premarital sex with him.

• Whoever else God brings to mind, no matter how insignificant that person or incident may seem to you.

You may be surprised. Your list may be longer than you expected. God may bring to mind people you haven't thought of for a long time. *Don't* be discouraged. This is good. The Bible reminds us that our hearts can easily deceive us into thinking we're better off than we really are. Often we minimize events and the effects they have in our lives. But God knows everything and everyone who has hurt us, and He wants us to be healed from it all.

Let's begin. Using the above list as a guide, follow these steps:

1. Ask God to bring to mind everyone you've had sexual contact with—voluntarily or involuntarily. Wait quietly, allowing God to bring names to memory.

2. Write every name on a piece of paper. If you don't know a name, write a description of the person or event.

3. Ask God to show you His perspective on each bond.

   a. If the bond was created through your own choice, ask God to show you why you participated, and the part you played.

   b. If the bond was created through someone else's choice forced on you, ask God to show you how that event affected you.

4. Pray that your heart will be humbled and your spirit contrite (see Psalm 51:17) so that you will experience true repentance. Please note: If you're praying for someone who has sexually

abused or raped you, you do not need to ask forgiveness for your violation of that person, because he or she violated you. However, you still need to ask God to sever the negative bond you've created with this person. And although you did not violate him or her, there may be something God brings to mind that you do need to ask forgiveness for—for example, perhaps you disobeyed your parents and dated someone who later abused you. God may show you that you need to ask forgiveness for disobeying your parents. Or He may show you that you've hurt Him by seeking love, attention, and affection from others rather than from Him. Although others are to blame for hurting us, your part may have been seeking love from the wrong places.[2]

5. Pray the following prayer with *each* name or incident:

Lord, I ask forgiveness for sinning against You and against my own body. In the name of Jesus, I sever and renounce the bonds I created with _____. I release my heart tie with this person physically, emotionally, and spiritually. I choose by faith to forgive _____ for his [or her] violation against me. Please forgive me of my violation against _____. Please remove the negative emotional baggage I've been carrying around with me. Restore to me a virgin heart—as though I'd never been with this person, and heal me completely of the damage this sin has caused me and my marriage. Thank You for Your forgiveness. I accept it fully.[3] Amen.

When you're done praying through your list, plan something to symbolize how this part of your life is now finished. It's forgiven, gone, buried, no longer able to impact your present life. You can burn your papers, tear them up, throw them away. You get the idea. Be creative. And get ready to feel lighter now that you're carrying a lot less weight.

If your husband is going through these steps with you, pray separately through your own lists first. After you've each prayed through your own list, plan for some uninterrupted, quiet time together. Take turns sharing your lists, being sure to only reveal the details that you've previously agreed to reveal. End your time praying together, thanking God for breaking the hold your past has had on you and for His blessing on your marriage.

Praying with Godly Sorrow

Godly sorrow is an important piece of your healing. What is godly sorrow? "Godly sorrow brings repentance that leads to salvation and leaves no regret, but worldly sorrow brings death" (2 Corinthians 7:10). I never knew there were two kinds of sorrow. I now realize that my sorrow was worldly for much of my life. Worldly sorrow is about me. I feel bad for what I've done and want to feel better. I want God to take it all away so I don't have to live in conflict or shame anymore. Worldly sorrow is about how the situation affects me or how it makes me look.

For example, when I gossip about someone, I'm instantly convicted. If I feel worldly sorrow, I am concerned about that person finding out what I said about him or her, and how that will make *me* look. In contrast, if I feel godly sorrow I'm concerned not about how my sin makes me look, but about how I've hurt others. I'm concerned about how I've tainted someone else's reputation, and I want to make it right so that person will look better, not so I'll look better. Worldly sorrow is focused inward; godly sorrow is focused outward.

When I first prayed through my list, I prayed with worldly sorrow. Although I knew that I had willingly consented to sex, with self-righteous judgment I felt the guys had the greater share of the responsibility and therefore the greater guilt. I was praying through each person without much feeling. It didn't seem to be working—at least not the way I'd expected. But halfway through my list, I began to see what God saw. For the first time I saw His perspective on my sin, on my choices. They weren't merely poor choices; they were wrong choices, sinful choices. Not only had I sinned against these guys—used them for my pleasure, to make me feel loved and treasured—I'd also sinned against God. Instead of going to Him to fill my need for love and acceptance, I'd gone to men, rejecting God's offer to fulfill my heart's deepest longings. I'd hurt not just myself and the men I'd used; I'd also hurt God.

Did you know that we can hurt God? When we reject Him, turn our backs on Him, go our own way, we cause Him pain. Imagine if your child—whom you've sacrificed everything for, loved, and cared for his or her whole life—were to suddenly and without provocation spurn your love, turn his or her back on you, and run away. Wouldn't that hurt? Maybe you already know the depth of this pain in your life. That's how God feels, but with even more intensity. Because He created us, gave up His life for us, wants to know us intimately and spend forever with us. We hurt Him when we look to others to meet our needs. We cause Him pain when we go our own way, turn our back on His love. When you feel the pain you've caused others and God because of your sin, you'll experience godly sorrow.

Godly sorrow, as 2 Corinthians 7:10 says, brings repentance with no regret. Godly sorrow allows us to turn away from that sin, to never want to do it again. When we finally realize the pain we've caused others and God, we're so disgusted with it that we never want to partake again.

Worldly sorrow, in contrast, only makes us feel worse about ourselves, causing us to sin again and again. Henry Cloud and John Townsend express it well in *How People Grow:*

> When we realize we are hurting someone we love, we change.
> Love and empathy change us. We treat others as we would want
> to be treated. Love constrains us. But guilt [worldly sorrow]
> actually causes sin to increase. It does not keep anyone in check.
> It only makes people rebel more. As Paul says [in Romans 5:20;
> 7:5] the law causes sin to increase.[4]

When I tasted godly sorrow, I began to weep. Really weep. With intense sorrow I wept for how I'd hurt these men, undermined their marriages, and inhibited their chance for intimacy with their future wives. And I wept for how I'd hurt God. He'd waited for me to come to Him, but I never came. Instead, I went to men, to sex—a cheap imitation of the love and intimacy God had waiting for me, longed to give me. Consequently, I knew I needed to go back to the beginning of my list and pray through the first half with the same godly sorrow that filled my prayers through the second half.

My greatest sorrow was for my husband. I now saw that the sex we'd had before marriage had robbed him of me, the real me. It had robbed us of the kind of emotional and physical intimacy God wanted for our marriage. My past sexual bonds and pain had caused me to resent my husband and treat him as the enemy. How sad. Eric was my life partner, the one who loved me the most on this earth, and yet I had so often scorned his love, leaving him to wonder what he'd done to be treated so badly. I couldn't imagine the pain I'd caused the one I loved so dearly.

GETTING RID OF TANGIBLE REMINDERS

Prayer is the first step in breaking sexual bonds; getting rid of tangible reminders is the second. With your prayers you took a step of faith. You prayed with faith that God would untie you from your past. Although we don't know for sure how He does it, we feel the result. God, in His miraculous, mysterious ways, severs the bonds we've created and brings healing. We can't explain it, but we know it has happened.

God's work is done on the inside, unseen, while our work is done on the outside, with the things we can see. One of the ways past lovers are kept alive for us is in tangible reminders—pictures, letters, music, gifts. Although they may seem insignificant, tangible objects can be conscious and subconscious reminders of past lovers. They can keep the memories and attachment alive, causing flashbacks and dreams. I'm not even sure how saving things keeps the attachment alive; I just know it does. That's why it's important to get rid of any reminders of past lovers. And I know that, for whatever reason, God cares about this action too. He uses our obedience in this, coupled with what He does for us spiritually, to break past bonds.

Carmen had a large orange trunk in her garage. In it were mementos of her earlier life, the one she was asking God to heal, the one full of pain, shame, and multiple sexual partners. She hadn't looked inside the trunk in decades. In fact, it was locked, and she had no idea where the key was. She'd decided not to worry about the trunk because it was far back on a shelf in her garage, and she never looked at it anyway. On the day she was asking God to show her the tangible reminders He wanted her to remove, she happened to clean out an old drawer. In it she found a small cloth bag, and inside the bag was the key to her trunk. A coincidence? An accident? Hardly. It was no accident that on that particular day she would stumble across the very thing she needed to rid herself of her past: a key she hadn't seen in years and thought she had lost. But God knew.

Whenever I meet with opposition regarding this important step (and I do), I remember what God did for Carmen. She had decided not to bother with the trunk, but God had other plans. The trunk had a crucial role in her breaking free from her past, and He didn't want her to miss out. The same goes for you.

Taking this step requires faith that God will do what He's promised. It also requires action. When we do something in response to what God is asking, it communicates that, although we don't understand, we're going to trust that God does. And though we don't see the reason at the time, we're trusting that what we do is part of His plan for our healing. The Bible says that God is pleased by our faith. Nothing pleases Him more than when we're willing to trust Him with the unseen. Our faith gives Him permission to unleash His power into our lives in ways that go beyond what we could ever have imagined.

Lisa knows this firsthand. She left her husband to move in with her lesbian lover. Four years later, after becoming a Christian, she began seeking healing from her sexual past. About two weeks into our study, she called me. She sounded frantic as she told me that she was attracted to one of the women in the group. She thought she needed to leave the group. I disagreed, feeling that if she wanted God to completely heal her, she needed to stay in a safe, godly environment that could help her heal. Running away would only send her back in despair to a lifestyle she assumed she'd never escape.

But I set some boundaries for her. She wasn't to sit near, touch, or communicate with this woman outside the group. I also assumed that something about this other woman's appearance was triggering in Lisa memories of past lovers, so I asked the other woman to change her appearance when she came to the group. Lisa worried that she'd never be able to have what she called a "regular" girl friendship, one that wasn't sexual. But upon learning about sexual bonding and how her early exposure to same-sex pornography had contributed to her attraction to women, she had hope that the God who'd created her could also heal her completely.

I asked Lisa if there was anything in her home that could keep the attachment to her lesbian lifestyle alive. As she thought a moment, she remembered a leather jacket hanging in her garage. She walked by it every day. I suggested that she get rid of the jacket, which she did. Lisa remained a part of the Bible study, and God did an amazing work of healing in her life. So much so that just two weeks ago Lisa remarried her husband. She sent me pictures, saying, "You are part of this miracle."

A miracle indeed. One the world says is impossible. But God knows otherwise and is waiting to show you a miracle just like it. In an e-mail, Lisa reflected on her healing, noting, "I was completely freed from that aspect of my former life.... I see her [the other woman from our study] on occasion at church and now have completely pure thoughts and feelings toward her!"

Are you ready for this next step toward healing? Once again spend some quiet time with God. Read and pray through the following list, asking God to remind you of anything that is keeping you unconsciously attached to past lovers:

- Ask God to bring to mind tangible reminders of past lovers: gifts, pictures, cards, jewelry, clothing, music, movies, letters, e-mails, phone numbers, furniture, and so on. Remove these items from your home. Throw out pictures, letters, and the like. You can give gifts, clothing, and jewelry to someone you don't see in your daily life or to your local Goodwill store.

- Break off any friendships with past lovers. Often friendship with a past lover can lead to an affair. If you want to completely sever your bond with that person, you must end the relationship.

- Consider what you're watching, reading, or listening to that triggers thoughts of past lovers. Movies, soap operas, magazines, sexually suggestive songs, or romance novels can all evoke thoughts of your past.

- Think about the people you associate with. If they do not contribute to the health and purity of your marriage, you need to find new friends.

- Examine emotional connections you have with men other than your spouse. Ask God to show you any emotional affairs or close friends of the opposite sex who are taking away from the intimacy in your marriage and could tempt you to have a physical affair.

- Ask God if there is something else not listed here that is keeping your attachment to the past alive.

Please note: If you're breaking a bond with an ex-husband with whom you've had children, some exceptions need to be made to this list. It's important for your kids to have pictures of their father, so you shouldn't get rid of pictures—including your wedding photos. These are part of your children's heritage, and it's important for them to have pictures for their own memories. Also keep gifts or anything else from your ex-husband that may remind your children of him in a special way. You may want to give them to your children when they're older. Be sure to ask God what is important to keep and what is appropriate to throw away. My first husband and I didn't have children, so I removed every-thing that reminded me of him—even my favorite, and I mean favorite, leather jacket that never went out of style.

DEALING WITH THE MEMORIES

While you can ask God to break past bonds and you can remove phys-ical reminders, you can't erase memories. But when you go through these steps, the memories won't have the same hold on you. That's been true for Lily, Carmen, and Lisa, and it has also been true for me. Since I broke the bonds to past lovers, my memories of them, while not elim-inated, have become vague, distant. Before I was healed, I could think of them without much effort and remember locations, activities, faces. Now remembering takes effort. Conjuring up their faces or how they made me feel is much harder and no longer worth the effort.

Nonetheless, there will be times when memories of past lovers will pop into your head. What should you do? Believe it or not, we can con-trol our thoughts. Sometimes it feels like they control us, but God has given us an amazing weapon to wield against unwanted thoughts. It's found in 2 Corinthians 10:3–5: "For though we live in the world, we do not wage war as the world does. The weapons we fight with are not the weapons of the world. On the contrary, they have divine power to demolish strongholds. We demolish arguments and every pretension that sets itself up against the knowledge of God, and we take captive every thought to make it obedient to Christ."

Did you catch that? God has given us a weapon that has divine power to demolish, destroy, and eliminate the strongholds in our lives. Unwanted thoughts can be a stronghold. They may not be strongholds initially, but when we welcome a thought in, let it take up residence, and begin to dwell on it, we gradually give it more and more control. It can take charge not only of our thoughts but of our attitudes and actions as well.

Let's say you get an unwanted lustful thought, such as fantasizing about having sex with someone not your spouse. The Bible says the Enemy and our own evil desires are responsible for the temptations we experience. The thought itself is not a sin. It is a temptation. I've heard many women say that they'd already sinned with the first thought, seeking to rationalize why they continued to act on it. But that's not true. The initial thought is not the sin but the temptation. What we do with the thought determines whether we let the temptation lead us to sin. When we welcome that thought in, dwell on it, and then act on it, it's gone from temptation to sin.

We can brandish the weapon God has given us to win against tempting thoughts the moment the unwanted thought comes in. It sounds too simple to be effective, but I've discovered that God means business when it comes to His divine warfare. What is this weapon? Taking every thought captive and making it obedient to Christ. How does it work? The moment you have a thought that you know is not right, pure, or godly, pray and ask God to take that thought captive and replace it with His truth.

Let's say you remember an impure moment with an ex-lover. The moment you realize this is not a thought you should have, pray, *Lord, I take this thought captive and give it to You. I want my thoughts to be obedient to Your will. Please replace this thought right now with Your truth.* You've just unleashed God's divine power to demolish the tempting power of this thought.

In addition, there may be something you're reading, watching, listening to, or participating in that is making you vulnerable to tempting thoughts. If so, stop what you're doing and do something else, so as not to fall victim again to this same thought. If you're lying down when the thought comes, get up, go for a walk, or read your Bible. If you're watching something that is sexually arousing for you, turn it off and read a book instead. If you're listening to music, turn it off or change the channel. You get the picture. God is the One with the power, but He's also given us common sense to recognize when things are triggering unwanted thoughts for us. The more you practice this, the better you'll get at it—just as you get better at anything else with practice. The more you resist, the more God's power is unleashed in you and the stronger your "thought-resisting muscles" become.

This method works for all kinds of unwanted thoughts, not just impure ones. I find God faithful when I have thoughts of fear, jealousy, anger, or self-doubt, when I start listening to lies the Enemy tries to tell me about myself, and so on. To be honest, I thought it was too good to be true and too simple to work. It's not. Although I don't feel an instant jolt of God's power, I'll realize within a few moments of turning from an unwanted thought that I'm not thinking about that person anymore, or that my fear, sadness, or anger is gone. Don't take my word for it; try it out yourself. There's nothing quite like having all the power of the God of the universe only a prayer away.

FORGIVING THOSE WHO HARMED US

One last thing. Remember those anger letters you wrote? I'd like you to write each person a forgiveness letter. You may not feel forgiveness for that person yet, but that's okay. Nowhere in the Bible does God say you need to *feel* forgiveness in order to forgive someone. In fact, the opposite is true. When we forgive by an act of our will, the feelings follow.

I'm not saying it's going to be easy or that the feelings of forgiveness happen right away. It takes time, especially if we've been severely wounded. But by not forgiving, we continue to allow those who have hurt us to mistreat us—maybe not physically but emotionally. Forgiveness is not for their benefit, but for ours. When we forgive we break the hold others have over our emotions, our hearts, our souls. Without forgiveness, we won't move forward. Without forgiveness we won't heal.

You may be asking, "If forgiveness is so important, how's it done?" Or, "How do I know I've forgiven them?" I learned this lesson a few summers ago when my husband and I were deeply wounded by friends. God showed me that when He teaches us in Matthew 18:21–22 to forgive the same person seventy-seven times (the large number is symbolic and refers to continual forgiveness), He also means forgiving them seventy-seven times for one offense. In other words, although our friends' offense was a one-time event, I had to forgive them numerous times before I felt forgiveness, before I was free of the hurt. Whenever my wounded emotions would well up, making me feel angry, hurt, and resentful, I'd repeat the words, usually out loud, *Lord, I choose to forgive _____ for _____. Now I trust you to give me the feelings of forgiveness.* My decision to forgive was repeated many times over several months. Eventually I noticed that I was feeling differently about them. Thoughts of them no longer caused painful feelings to surface. I obeyed God and made the choice to forgive. But He's the One who made it happen.

A word of clarification: Forgiveness does not mean you condone the harm done to you or that you need to reconcile the relationship—especially if the person refuses to acknowledge his or her actions, is unrepentant, or continues to be unhealthy or harmful to you. In fact, forgiveness may involve allowing that individual to suffer the necessary consequences of his or her actions. When you forgive others, you allow God to heal you, and you give Him an opportunity to work in their lives too.

THROUGH THE HARDEST PART

How're you doing? The last three chapters have been a lot to absorb. Up to this point we've been mainly focusing on you. On your past, your healing. As we move forward, we'll see how God's healing in your life will make you a new wife, mother, leader, and friend. The hardest part is over. Now get ready for God to unleash His healing power through you to those around you.

Become Your Husband's
Best Friend

"First comes love, then comes marriage, then comes a baby in the baby carriage." If you're from my era, you may remember this little rhyme. It's based on the truth that lasting love grows out of a deep friendship, which makes a sure foundation for marriage. When a man and a woman become friends first and save sex for marriage, sex enhances the intimacy that's already been established.

But many of us reversed the order. We became lovers first, without developing a friendship. And as I mentioned in chapter 4, sex becomes the glue for the relationship, short-circuiting the opportunity for friendship. When lovers get married and the newness subsides, we discover that we need more than sex to feel close. We need to be good friends. If that was the case for you and your husband, you can still become best friends if you both are willing; you can grow in intimacy.

Are you and your husband friends? Are you able to talk about things that matter to you? to your marriage? In their book *Intimate*

Encounters, David and Teresa Ferguson and Chris and Holly Thurman describe three dimensions of a marriage relationship—physical, emotional, and spiritual.[1] A healthy marriage nurtures all three. How healthy is your marriage?

Take a moment to reflect on your marriage's health—its physical, emotional, and spiritual health. If your husband has expressed a desire to support you on this journey, invite him to join you in this exercise. Answer the questions separately, and then spend time sharing your answers with each other. If you're doing this exercise alone, you'll find that as you heal and God leads you to share more with your husband, you'll be prepared with greater insight into your marriage and with just the right words to say.

Write a response to these two questions for each level of intimacy: How well do you relate with each other on this level? What needs to change or improve in this level?

Physical

_____

_____

_____

Emotional

_____

_____

_____

Spiritual

_____

_____

_____

Reflecting on the health of your marriage and what you'd like to see improve will help you articulate your needs and desires with your husband, which is a necessary step in developing deeper intimacy. It can also help you discern the path you need to take to achieve the healthy goals you desire for your marriage. For example, if you determine that your spiritual health needs to improve, you may decide to initiate praying together, reading the Bible at a meal, or attending church more regularly. If your emotional intimacy needs healing, you may decide to see a marriage counselor or schedule more time for each other, such as by scheduling regular date nights.

DON'T BE AFRAID

I don't know where you are in your marriage right now. But I'm sure that, if you're reading this, you have a desire for something better, something more, in your relationship with your spouse. Regardless of what level of intimacy you've attained, there's always room for growth and improvement.

But if you're like many of the wives I've counseled, you may be afraid to take emotional risks with your husband because of things that have happened in the past. You've tried being vulnerable and sharing your heart with him before. But rather than increasing intimacy, your efforts caused fighting, anger, greater distance. I understand how sharing at this deeper level with your spouse may cause anxiety and fear.

But don't be afraid. Attaining greater intimacy does involve risk, even the risk of being hurt, rejected, or misunderstood again. But remember that you aren't the same person you were before you started the healing process. Healing gives you newfound courage. How so?

First, healing allows you to be okay with who you are. You no longer feel the weight of meeting everyone else's needs or being responsible for the moods and behavior of others. You now know you won't be destroyed if what you share makes others angry or unhappy. You can give people permission to accept responsibility for their own choices, even for how they respond to you. And you see others differently. No longer self-absorbed with your pain, you can now see how the angry responses of others are not so much about you but about their own pain and fear.

Second, you no longer look to others to meet your needs. You've discovered that God is the One who loves you unconditionally and will meet every need you have for love, acceptance, and approval.

Healing will allow unconditional love and forgiveness to flow through you, enabling you to release your husband from the impossible burden of having to meet all your needs. Your vulnerability will come across as confidence and strength. Your new openness will allow him to feel safe, encouraging him to open up with you. The walls will begin to crumble between you as love and intimacy grow.

But even when their wives change and become more open and responsive, some husbands are not willing to do the same. Instead they respond with anger or resentment. If this is your husband, I encourage you to persevere. Ask God to show you what's behind your husband's angry and tough exterior. Has he been hurt? Is he afraid of something? Have you spurned his loving advances for so long that he no longer trusts you? What has happened in his past or in your marriage that has caused him to be distant emotionally? Some men were raised in a culture that discouraged the soft, tender side of men. What was modeled for him? How did his father treat him? How have *you* treated him?

You may not be able to trust your husband yet, but you can trust God with him. God changed you; He can change your mate. So if you don't immediately get the response you long for, trust that as you continue to obey God, He'll do the work needed in your husband's heart.

Most important, don't stop letting God soften and heal you. As He does, your transformation will be undeniably evident, and you will become a living witness to His power in your life. Even if your husband isn't ready to walk this journey yet, the steps offered here can still benefit you, and the changes in you will help your marriage and other relationships. Continue to tell your husband what God is teaching you about *you*. Tell him how your sexual past has caused you to respond negatively toward him with regard to sex. Or how the wounds from your past have caused you to withdraw from him emotionally and physically, keeping you from loving and respecting him, from turning your heart toward him. Use this opportunity to express your regret for your part in your marital struggles and to ask for his forgiveness. Resist the urge to tell him what needs to change in him. He will oppose being "fixed," especially if he believes you're the problem, or if you are trying to make him change. Remember, while your husband shares part of the responsibility for what is going on in your marriage, God isn't starting with him—He's starting with you.

Assessing the Level of Emotional Intimacy in Your Marriage

In chapter 4 we talked about the five levels of emotional intimacy. At what level do you think you and your husband are right now? Remember, true intimacy happens when both are at the same level, communicating with equal depth and vulnerability. If you are communicating at level four, with feelings, and your husband responds at level three, with opinions or beliefs, you won't feel heard or understood.

In order to talk about what matters, both partners need to communicate at the two highest levels of intimacy—sharing experiences and feelings and expressing needs and desires. If you're not there yet, don't worry. You can be. But it won't happen overnight. Deeper intimacy takes time. As you heal, your husband will see the positive changes in you. If he is like many of the husbands of the women I know who have gone through healing, he'll want to know more about what you're learning and may even join you on your journey.

Although we may move between the levels at different times in our marriage, our relationship is usually characterized by the one level we gravitate toward most of the time.

Take a moment to assess which level you and your husband are at right now. Consider the five levels of emotional intimacy listed below.

- Level One: Safe Communication (factual information)
- Level Two: Others' Opinions and Beliefs
- Level Three: Personal Opinions and Beliefs
- Level Four: My Feelings and Experiences (our background, goals, feelings, dreams, failures, joy, pain)
- Level Five: My Needs, Emotions, and Desires (our needs, desires, emotional reactions)

1. At which level do you generally communicate with your husband? At which level do you believe your husband generally communicates with you? (Look back at chapter 4 for a more detailed description of these levels.)

_____

_____

_____

_____

2. What is holding you back from the next level of intimacy? How do you think your husband would answer this question?

_____

_____

_____

_____

3. What needs to happen in your relationship so that you can communicate at a higher level? How do you think your husband would answer this question? (If you've invited your husband to join you on this journey, discuss the answers to these questions together.)

_____

_____

_____

_____

_____

Using these questions to assess your current level of intimacy will give you insight into how to proceed to the next level. Since you're married, I assume that you will have reached at least the third level, where you're sharing your opinions and beliefs. You may occasionally, briefly, move to the fourth level and even the fifth level but then retreat back to the third level—your nonthreatening safe zone, where you feel comfortable. The questions assume that you're currently communicating at the third level and will help you move into the fourth level, and then the fifth level of communication.

HELP FOR GROWING CLOSER

If you and your spouse haven't been able to share heartfelt needs and emotions, the thought of talking about things that are more intimate may make you feel uneasy. When a relationship has subsisted on superficial nonemotional communication, broaching deeper issues may seem awkward, even unpleasant. But don't worry. You're not alone. And communicating at a deeper level doesn't take special skill; it just takes practice. And a little courage. If you'll trust God for the courage, I have some conversation starters to give you the practice.

My goal is to help generate meaningful conversation that allows you both to learn more about each other. But rather than beginning by talking about yourself, show interest in what your husband has to say by asking questions of him. This demonstrates your love and care for him, and nothing can melt a heart or break down a wall of hostility faster than knowing someone cares about you and how you feel. True intimacy, real conversation, flows both ways. So although you're initiating conversation by asking him questions, the goal is that both of you will share your feelings, thoughts, and emotions. After he answers your question, ask him, "Would you like to know how I'd answer that question?" Since you have listened to him, he may be eager to listen to you.

Be patient. Your husband may not respond the way you want or expect at first. If this is new territory for your marriage, he will need time to absorb this new person you're becoming. Give him time to process how he truly feels and time to practice expressing it accurately. Most important: don't get defensive. Easier said than done, I know. Jumping to our own defense is natural. But defensiveness often comes out of fear and pride, causing conversation to shut down or, worse, escalate to a fight—something I know from personal experience. So before you initiate conversation, ask God to help you keep silent when your husband answers, regardless of how much his response hurts. And after you've listened, answer with humility and kindness—two things that God promises will help dispel anger and circumvent a fight.

One last word of advice: if your husband is like mine, he can only talk about feelings for so long. So don't bombard him with the whole list all at once. Start with one question, and allow the conversation to flow naturally from there. With practice you'll find that you and your husband will be comfortable with longer periods of more intimate conversation.

Moving from Level Three to Level Four

Here are some conversation starters:

1. How can I pray for you today? (This is a great question to begin with. If it's been a while since you shared intimate conversation, you may want to stay on this question for a few days before getting deeper. You might ask him this question every day for a week or two to help open him up for more intimate conversation. Don't feel rejected if he has nothing to say at first. Gently persevere.)
2. What is the greatest joy in your life right now? What's the greatest struggle in your life right now?
3. In what areas do you feel our marriage is doing well? In what areas do you feel we need to improve?
4. What's your greatest worry right now?
5. What do you feel God has been speaking to you about lately?
6. How have I hurt you recently? or ever in our marriage?
7. What scares you most about the future? What are you looking forward to in the future?
8. What is something from your past you've never shared with me?
9. What do you regret most about your past?
10. What in your past has had the most positive influence on who you are today?

It may take some time for your husband to feel comfortable answering these questions and for mutual level-four communication to occur. Give it time. When he responds positively to questions like these and does his best to answer them and then ask them of you, it's a good indication that he is willing to move to the next level of intimacy with you.

MOVING FROM LEVEL FOUR TO LEVEL FIVE

As you begin to feel safe communicating with each other at the fourth level, you'll be encouraged to navigate the next level of intimacy—the highest, or fifth, level. Invite your husband to continue this journey to deeper intimacy by saying, "The closer we get, the safer I feel with you and the more I feel loved by you. This allows me to trust you more and want to give more of myself to you, emotionally and physically." In other words, the more emotional intimacy you feel, the more desire you'll have for your husband and for sex. This next exercise will help you talk honestly with each other about your deepest longings, needs, and desires in your marriage.

1. Ask your husband how you make him feel as a man, as a husband, as a father.

2. Ask him what you can do to improve how you make him feel in the above areas.

3. Ask him to join you in making a list of everything a healthy marriage needs in order to thrive. Your list might include needs such as affection, romance, intimacy, respect, security, attention, approval, love, trust, or fun.

4. Use the list to discuss what each of your top three to five needs are.

5. Now share with each other how well you feel your needs are being met in your marriage.

6. If some of your needs aren't being met, discuss together what you can do to improve in this area.

7. Make a list of your deepest desires for yourself, your spouse, and your marriage. Take turns sharing your desires with each other.

8. Take turns sharing something the other has done to deeply hurt you in your marriage. Make sure you ask forgiveness of each other for the hurts you've caused.

9. Take turns sharing what the other has done to make you feel loved, safe, and cared for. Make it a regular habit to reflect on what your husband does well and to praise him for it.

SHARING THE SECRET OF INFIDELITY

People often ask me, "Do I need to tell my spouse about my past affair(s)?" That may be a question on your mind as well. Not having experienced this personally, I want to tell you what God has taught me as I've helped others deal with this issue.

Emotional and physical affairs are common among women who've had sex in their pasts, especially if they've endured sexual abuse or trauma. In fact, every woman I've talked with who's had an affair has had some kind of abuse or rape in her past. I realize this isn't always the case, but in my experience, women with abusive pasts are more likely to engage in extramarital affairs. Why is that? There are many factors that can lead to an affair. Let me address a few of them here.

Wounding from sexual abuse and trauma causes women to shut down emotionally in marriages, and they feel lonely and detached from their husbands. This can make them vulnerable to attention from other men or women. The lack of trust and intimacy in their marriages makes emotional intimacy with someone else more enticing. Once these women have connected emotionally, they'll be susceptible to physical intimacy.

Early exposure to sex as a child or young teen can lead to sexual addiction and promiscuous behavior, even after marriage. In addition, without healing, women who've been abused or raped have a greater chance of being victimized again. They have difficulty standing up for and protecting themselves. Those in an affair may feel they are trapped in a relationship they didn't initiate or want, yet they are afraid or unable to end it. They can be easy targets for sexual predators and often minimize potential danger. One woman who'd been traumatically raped at the age of thirteen told me that whenever she argued with her husband, she'd drive around aimlessly at night, finally ending up at a bar by herself and not coming home for hours. When I expressed my concern for her safety when she was alone in a bar at night, she was surprised. She'd never once thought about the danger.

And, of course, there's the bonding factor. The sex women had before marriage inhibits their ability to bond completely with their spouses, making it easier to betray them with someone else. Also, without oxytocin keeping the "wow" of sex alive when their chemical response diminishes, these women can experience sexual withdrawal from their husbands, which causes them to seek sexual excitement with someone else. Although I'm mainly speaking from a woman's perspective regarding affairs, I believe that sexual addictions, sexual withdrawal, and emotional detachment are some of the reasons men have affairs as well.

The affair, with the secret shame you suffer, is one of those walls keeping you from the highest level of intimacy. Do you remember Sophie from chapter 3, who told her husband about her multiple affairs? Before she came through healing, she had no intention of telling him. She was ashamed, and she was afraid of his angry reaction. She thought he'd leave her. But God showed her that this secret was coming between them and that they'd never have the kind of intimacy she desired unless she confessed her affairs to him. Even though the last affair had happened eight years earlier, her shame was so great that she could barely look her husband in the eye. She struggled with kissing him on the mouth—the most intimate of touches. And they rarely had sex.

God doesn't want us to have secrets. We don't have any with Him, because He knows everything we've ever done and loves us anyway. When we keep secrets from our spouses, the Enemy uses the secrets to condemn us, torment us with shame, and keep us isolated. Secrets cause your husband pain also. Your husband knows there's something wrong and may assume that he's the problem. It's a lonely, painful burden to bear. Confessing our sins to each other leads to healing (see James 5:16). Plus, confessing protects us from future affairs. Ironically, the shame we feel from our affairs and the emotional distance our shame imposes make us susceptible to repeating the offense. Confession opens a door to greater intimacy—exactly what we long for and need in order to resist being tempted again.

Alfred Ells, counselor and author of *Restoring Innocence,* wrote:

> Secrets and shame from the past hinder the oneness and intimacy that healthy marriages require.... The Scriptures refer to marriage as being one flesh, naked and not ashamed. For oneness to exist, nakedness or total baring of one's self is necessary.... It is the confession of our sinfulness that brings release to the shame. That which we fear is what we must face in order to be healed. The hidden territory will remain a stumbling block to us and to intimacy until we are willing to risk

its exposure. And uncleansed shame creates codependent and compulsive sex.[2]

Although Sophie and her husband had to walk through a painful time after she confessed, it was a healing, restoring pain that drew them closer. The intimacy and closeness they have now is dramatically different from what they had experienced before her confession. Neither one regrets the process, despite how painful it was, because their love and marriage were reborn as a result.

"That may be all right for them, but is it right for me?" you may be asking. I know: it's scary. But if God is leading you to tell your spouse, He will not only guide you regarding when and how to tell, but He will also prepare your spouse for what you have to say. You must seek guidance from God, not only about what to tell, but also about how and when. When we do it God's way, in His time, we minimize the damage and maximize the healing from the confession. As you prepare to tell your spouse about an affair, consider these points.

What to Do Before You Tell

Before you have a conversation with your spouse:

- *Pray, pray, pray.* Pray before you do or say anything.
- *Wait on God for the right time and place to tell your spouse.* You may have a sense of urgency and want to share your secrets right away. Pray and ask if you're following God's leading or just wanting to get something off your chest. If God is leading you, it will be with the other person's well-being in mind. When we do it from selfish motives, we won't be as sensitive to the other person's feelings. God will let you know if and when

you should tell your spouse. You may already be feeling God nudge you in this area. That doesn't mean you're supposed to tell your spouse right away. Continue to pray and wait on God for the right time and place. When we do it in His time, He prepares those He wants us to tell.

When I was getting ready to tell my children about my past, I decided to sit them all down together and tell them at once. It was mainly out of selfishness, because I couldn't imagine telling my story four times. But when I prayed about it, I realized that God had a different plan. He was thinking of my children, whereas I was thinking about me. Instead God wanted me to tell them individually so that they could process what I had to say alone, not with everyone there. As I waited on God for the right moment, He let me know it was time when my daughter unexpectedly said one day, "Mom, I think there are some things about your past you're not sharing with us." Women have told me that just as they were thinking of telling their husbands about an affair, their husbands started having random dreams about their wives having an affair.

- *Get wise counsel.* Before Sophie told her husband, she got counsel from me and another trusted counselor who also knew her husband. One thing he suggested was that she wait until after the holidays so that their happy family memories wouldn't be marred by the pain of the confession. It was wise advice that she heeded.

Talk with a professional counselor or trusted Christian leader or mentor before you proceed. As Sophie discovered, wise counsel can keep you from causing your spouse more pain than you need to. Counselors and mentors can also confirm what God is saying to you and help you proceed with wisdom.

What to Do If Your Marriage Is Rocky

Although full disclosure of a past affair is essential for ultimate oneness and intimacy in a marriage, there are times in a relationship when the disclosure may make things worse. Prayer and wise counsel from a professional should be heeded to help you determine if your marriage or spouse is currently not in a healthy place to receive what you have to say. Alfred Ells wrote in *Restoring Innocence* that when it comes to current affairs, however, you have no choice but to confess them, regardless of the state of your marriage.[3] Not only will exposure help break the affair's hold on you, but it also will be the catalyst for repairing your marriage.

What to Say

This confession will be one of the hardest things you've ever had to say to someone, especially someone you love. I understand if you're unsure how to begin. You might say, "There is something I need to tell that you that I'm so ashamed of and that I regret more than anything I've ever done because I know it's going to hurt you. But I want you to know that this has nothing to do with you or how much I love you. This is about something that's very broken in me." Then tell your spouse what you need to say. Afterward tell him how sorry you are and that you are asking for forgiveness.

If the affair was in the past, let him know that you've been faithful since that time. If it's a current affair, tell him you've broken it off, you love him, and you want to heal your marriage. If you were abused or raped or exposed to sex early in your life and God has shown you how your past made you vulnerable to the affair, share that with your spouse. It will be important for him to know this is about you, not him. Plus it will give him assurance that healing will ensure your future faithfulness.

Don't be alarmed if he doesn't say "I forgive you" right away. That may take time. Be humble, kind, compassionate, and patient. And trust God with the results.

How Much to Say

When Sophie first told her husband about her affairs, she said, "I have not been a faithful wife." She then went on to say that during a certain period in their marriage she'd had more than one affair. Over the next several days and weeks, her husband wanted to know more specific details. How many? Who? When? Were the children his? Under the advice of their counselor, she answered all of his questions as honestly as she could, never giving him more than he asked for at the time.

Your husband will be grieving as he processes what you've told him. You need to give him time and permission to do so without pressure to "get over it" quickly. Part of his grieving will include wanting to hear more details. Answer truthfully. Honesty is essential for increasing trust and intimacy in your marriage. But telling him only what he can hear at the time allows him to grieve gradually. This healthy progression through the grieving process gives him a chance to work through each piece of information in his time, not yours. It also protects him from details that he doesn't want to know or isn't ready to hear. Of course, you will want to get it all out so you don't have to tell it over and over, but this is not about you anymore. It's about helping your husband mourn and heal from your betrayal. His way, in his time.

What to Do After You've Told

Go together to a Christian marriage counselor. A good counselor can guide you both as you heal. Sophie and her husband saw a Christian marriage counselor for six months after she revealed her secret. He helped them heal and restore trust and intimacy in their marriage. Without this step, they would have spent considerably more time grieving, and might have wounded each other further in the process.

Although God desires that couples heal and that marriages are reconciled, He also gives people free choice. There's no guarantee how your spouse will respond. Just because God is leading you to share and you're choosing to obey doesn't mean there won't be consequences. But don't panic. God can do the impossible when we surrender it to Him. He uses many things to heal us, but time will be one of them.

The Sweetness of Emotional Oneness

There was a time in my marriage when I was afraid to talk about what mattered to me. Or to express my dislikes, needs, desires. But not anymore. Ephesians 2:14 offers a picture of what God has done, "For he himself is our peace, who has made the two one and has destroyed the barrier, the dividing wall of hostility." I didn't know I had a wall of hostility. But I did. My wall consisted of anger, resentment, old wounds, unrealized expectations, hurts, regrets, and more. The wall had separated my husband and me, making us two rather than one. Our newly dismantled wall doesn't mean we don't hurt each other anymore, but now when I get hurt I refuse to let the wall go back up. Present pain no longer triggers old wounds which would've previously caused me to shut down emotionally. I can now handle hurts head-on with grace, forgiveness, and maturity—without letting the hurts fester and collect into bricks of resentment. Now that I've tasted the sweetness of emotional oneness, staying wall free is something I strive for.

But emotional oneness takes work, as much of marriage does. God showed me that with my personality I need to actively pursue emotional closeness with others, even my husband. I tend to hold things in, process them myself. But that's not what marriage is about. God occasionally has to remind me of this when I'm turning inward, shutting Eric out. And then I purposefully open up and tell him things that are on my heart. It's a process that's well worth the effort, as you're soon to discover. Not only does it make two one, but as I and countless women have discovered, it also leads to more satisfying, fulfilling sex.

It's Time to Be Lovers Again

A s I grew emotionally closer to my husband, I became more responsive to having sex with him, because I felt safe, loved, heard. But what increased my *desire* for sex was changing my view of it. I discovered that the world's view of sex and God's view of it are radically different. The world thinks that great sex depends on the techniques between the sheets. But in discovering God's view, I've learned that becoming lovers again, reigniting desire, is not about the mechanics of sex as much as it is about trust, safety, and love. Great sex happens when we heal past and present hurts, enabling us to rebond emotionally, and then allowing God to replace the lies we've internalized about sex, ourselves, and men with His truth.

Instead, the world proclaims that the measure of great sex is in the act itself. Here are some examples of the titles you might find on any number of women's magazines:

- "The Hottest Sex Tips on the Planet"
- "New Sex Dos and Don'ts—How to Handle Anything Naked"

- "75 Crazy-Hot Sex Moves."
- "Hot (and Cold) New Sex Tricks."

Sex today has become less about love and intimacy and more about the method. It's more about the act in the moment, less about the relationship, and all about instant, selfish pleasure. Sexually explicit material, whether from pornography, media, TV, movies, or books, gets much of the blame, in my opinion. As it seeps into our eyes, ears, minds, and beds, it influences our expectations of sex for ourselves and others. It desensitizes us to what is normal or acceptable. It subliminally pushes us to riskier and more perverse acts in the name of sexual freedom and choice.

Those who have been fed our culture's view of sex in what they watch and listen to have a tainted, unfulfilling view of sex. It's a cheap, corrupt imitation of God's holy gift. It's a view that will lead to destruction of our lives (emotionally, spiritually, and physically), disappointment, and repeated relationship failure. Just thinking about it makes me sad and angry at the same time. I'm heartbroken as I sit with countless women of all ages whose lives have been damaged because someone else's perverted view of sex was imposed on them. And I'm angry because we've been robbed of the pure, selfless intimacy we wanted and that God planned for us in marriage.

WHY GOD GAVE US SEX

In their book *Intimate Issues,* Linda Dillow and Lorraine Pintus list six reasons God gave us sex. Yes, six. But the world has taken just one of those reasons, pleasure, and marketed it as the sole purpose for sex. God undoubtedly made sex pleasurable and wants us to enjoy it, but when we make pleasure our only purpose, we can use sex to hurt others.

Because sex becomes all about me—about my pleasure, in this moment. If we're not enjoying sex, or if sex with our current partner has lost its appeal, then sex has no purpose. So when all the tricks for better sex have failed, we'll either move on to someone new or, if we're married, we may stop having sex altogether. Pleasure is also why we selfishly pressure our spouses to do things that make them feel devalued or uncomfortable. Because it will make *us* feel good. Making sex only about pleasure has made women and children sexual victims and increased promiscuity, risky sex, and the number of broken marriages.

But I've got great news. God had many benefits in mind when He gave us sex. In addition to pleasure, according to Dillow and Pintus, the other benefits are to create life, for intimate oneness, for knowledge, as a defense against temptation, and for comfort.[1] Let's take a closer look at each of these.

God Gave Sex for Pleasure

There's no doubt that God intended for sex to be enjoyable. In addition to uniquely designing our bodies for procreation through sex, He also designed both males and females to experience orgasm during sex. This is a physiological response completely independent of any necessary physical function; it's simply for us to enjoy. To prove His point, He gave us an entire book in the Bible, Song of Songs, devoted to sexual love and intimacy in marriage. God used this book to transform my view of sex from the world's way to His way—and to change our marriage.

God Gave Us Sex to Create Life

I had the privilege of being present at my first grandchild's birth. I find it amazing that God would choose the sexual relationship as the means to procreate. In Genesis 1:28 He gives the command to "be fruitful and increase in number; fill the earth." Since there's only one way to do that, He's also telling us to have sex—lots of it, in marriage. The gift He gives in return is the reflection of our love in the faces and lives of our children.

But sex also brings life to our marriage relationship. God uses sex in marriage to bond us emotionally, spiritually, and physically. Sex nurtures our marriage, causing it to thrive and grow. It's like the vitamins we take each day to keep us healthy. (Don't worry, I'm not implying you need sex every day to stay healthy—regardless of what your husband has told you!) A sexless marriage creates emotional distance. We stop growing and thriving as a couple. Without sex we become roommates, living separate lives under the same roof. Like my plants that quickly wither without water in the California heat, sexless marriages will wither and die from inadequate nurture.

God Gave Us Sex for Intimate Oneness

The intimate oneness God had in mind in marriage encompasses every part of our being. God says that this bond is a mystery in the same way that becoming one with Him is a mystery (see Ephesians 5:31–32). It's not something we can do on our own. God is the one who takes two people and makes them one. Because sex creates this bond, He warns us not to become one with others, because that can hinder complete oneness with the one we marry.

God Gave Sex for Knowledge

As close as we as parents are to our children, we won't know them with the same intimate knowledge their spouses will. "Adam knew [*yadah*] Eve his wife, and she conceived and bore Cain" (Genesis 4:1, NKJV). In this verse the Hebrew word for sexual intercourse, *yadah*, means "to know someone at a deep, intimate level." It means a "knowing" of someone that no one else has. In marriage the more we have sex, the more we learn about our spouses, the closer we become, and the more we "know" them.

In Daniel 11:32 the same Hebrew word is used to describe the people's relationship with God—"the people who know their God." God equates our earthly oneness in sex to the supernatural oneness we have with Him—that's how seriously He views the sexual relationship.

No wonder the Enemy strives to destroy this area of our lives. What better way to attack us or our relationship with God. When we misuse sex, our relationship with Him is broken. Only through forgiveness and repentance (purposefully turning away from our sin) will our relationship with Him be restored. And only through healing and the breaking of past sexual bonds will we be able to unite with our spouses in the way God intended—with complete oneness.

God Gave Sex as a Defense Against Temptation

God designed sex in marriage to strengthen our bond by increasing our desire for each other and reducing the temptation of attraction to others. But when we neglect this part of our relationship, we can cause our emotional connectedness to wane. When our thoughts and hearts are not in tune, our attention can wander to others. First Corinthians 7:2, 5 says, "But since there is so much immorality, each man should have his own wife, and each woman her own husband.... Do not deprive each other except by mutual consent and for a time, so that you may devote yourselves to prayer. Then come together again so that Satan will not tempt you because of your lack of self-control."

When my husband and I took that sexual fast for a month, I discovered firsthand how sex was a gift of defense for my husband. Three weeks into our fast he mentioned being relieved that we only had one week to go. I assumed he meant that this was harder than he'd imagined, and he was excited for it to be over. Instead, he confessed that he'd begun to notice other women at work—something he'd not previously struggled with. It was discouraging for him, especially as he wanted to remain pure in his thoughts and desire for me. And it was a revealing lesson for me. The gift of sex I offer my husband ensures that his head and heart turns for me and me alone. It helps to keep his heart and mind pure, bringing sweet peace to the depths of his soul and erecting a wall of defense around our marriage.

God Gave Sex for Comfort

In 2 Samuel 12:24 God shows us through David how sex can be a selfless way to comfort our spouse. "Then David comforted his wife Bathsheba, and he went to her and lay with her. She gave birth to a son, and they named him Solomon." *Comforted* is used as a verb, or action word, in this verse. It indicates that the comforting act David did was to have sexual relations with his wife.

There was a time in our marriage when I went through a severe depression. Greatly incapacitated, I had to trust my husband to care for me in many ways. At the time I'd lost desire for everything in my life, including sex. One of my wisest decisions at this time was to trust my husband in the area of sex. Although I had no desire, I agreed to respond willingly to his attempts to comfort me through sex.

It's been sixteen years now since that event. Although it was a devastating and difficult time for us, what I remember most is the positive impact Eric's comfort had on me. I'm now aware that the chemicals and hormones we release during sex can reduce anxiety and stress and increase trust and emotional healing. I believe that in addition to medication and rest, God used my husband's gift of comfort sex to heal me. By its nature, depression makes one feel isolated and emotionally distant, which can weaken a marriage. An added benefit of our comfort sex was that it strengthened our bond, allowing us to survive what could have been a threat to our marriage.

But learning about God's view of sex wasn't the only thing that helped change my marriage and my feelings about sex. It also helped to simply have more sex.

More Sex, More Oxytocin, More Bonding, More Desire

"Just do it" is a popular slogan for Nike. Not only is the saying catchy and an effective marketing tool, it's also true. When we do something regardless of whether we feel like it at the time, it changes our attitude toward it.

The same is true of sex. Hard to believe, I know. But as we saw in chapter 2, personal experience and science concur. Anthropologist Helen Fisher, a professor at Rutgers School of Arts and Sciences in New Jersey, has spent most of her career studying the biochemical pathways of love. She confirms what others have discovered about the chemicals and hormones we release during sex that create attraction and attachment. Dr. Fisher said, "Assuming a fairly healthy relationship, if you have enough orgasms with your partner, you may become attached to him or her. You will stimulate oxytocin.... Massage [which means physical contact such as hugs, kisses, and caresses]. Make love. These things trigger oxytocin and thus make you feel much closer to your partner."[2]

Healing allows us to have regular sex with our husbands, which stimulates the production of oxytocin, which, in turn, gradually bonds us closer and closer. We feel loved, able to trust. As our view of sex and our husbands changes, we begin to have positive experiences with sex. Without the anxiety and stress our previous wall of defense produced, we can relax and enjoy our lovemaking.

Although we may not experience increased sexual desire (we'll discuss some reasons in chapter 12), we become responsive, no longer resisting sex or rejecting the advances of our husbands. We become willing participants of subsequent encounters. And the more and more we have sex, the closer we feel to our husbands. And with that bonding comes desire. For some, a desire for sex. But for most, a desire for our husbands…to be loved by them…to love them in return. The pleasure of sex, although needed and greatly appreciated, comes second to the emotional high we experience from being together. When we make intimacy, not pleasure, the primary goal of sex, everyone wins. Because pleasure is a natural outcome when we pursue true intimacy.

The married women I've worked with agree. With contagious enthusiasm they told me that after their healing everything changed in their relationships with their husbands. They saw themselves, their husbands, and sex in a new way. They felt more love for and from their husbands. They felt safe, bonded, connected, and more trusting and intimate with their husbands. They were less inhibited, felt more sexy, were more emotionally open and authentic. They experienced less stress and anxiety, held fewer grudges, and were more caring, loving, and forgiving to their husbands. And the best part? All of them said the sex was better. They could enjoy sex and even feel free to initiate it, much to the delight of their husbands.

And what about the husbands? Did they see changes? Would they agree with their wives? A resounding yes. One husband said that the changes he had already observed in his wife after just a few weeks into her journey toward healing gave him hope that his marriage would survive. Even though he had recently learned of his wife's infidelity, he chose to stay in the marriage and work things out.

Cindy's husband decided to go through the healing Bible study with her because of the changes he saw in her. It had been a hard year. He was out of work, and their primary car was totaled in an accident, but in spite of the extra pressure this put on their marriage, their relationship started to blossom. Each morning they went through the Bible study on their own, and then in the evening they discussed what they had learned that morning and prayed together. As Cindy's husband wrote out his story, God showed him things he'd forgotten. Wounds he'd buried. It led him to ask Cindy for forgiveness for encouraging her to abort their child. In a letter to her he wrote:

> I got you pregnant and buried my head in the sand. And when you asked for a decision, I took the easy way out—for me. I didn't consider you or your feelings. For this I am truly sorry. I should have been the man and not put you in this circumstance in the first place. I should have been there for you. If you find it in your heart, would you forgive me for damaging you?

Wow! She couldn't believe it. They'd never talked about this before. And then he did something she'd never seen him do. He cried. For the first time they talked and cried together about their baby. With forgiveness and healing for them both, the bitter residue is now gone. The result, Cindy says, has been incredible.

> We're talking about sex all the time now! We're learning to be open about our desires, dislikes, and hang-ups. I am finally able

to be present mentally with my husband when we have sex. There is no longer a huge barrier that I have to climb to be able to get to the point where I can "allow" sex. We're having daytime sex, on Sunday afternoons even! I no longer feel like I need to guard myself from sex, and I am learning to trust. It's given our sex life a lot more depth and joy. God is healing the shame and hurt of my past, restoring me and taking away the "filthy rags" feeling I've had and replacing it with His and my husband's love and acceptance of me.

But the greatest gift through all this (aside from the great sex) is the genuine bonding in our relationship. Our great relationship has become the prize, and the great sex, the frosting. I no longer feel robbed after sex, but loved and content.

This from a woman who came to me broken, angry, wounded, and rarely having sex. "I hope this helps someone, Barb," she told me. In fact, Cindy gave me her permission to tell her story in this book. That's what happens when shame is extinguished. The secrets are gone. Others knowing our name, our story—none of that matters anymore…as long as it can help even one other person find the same joy and healing we've found.

HIS TIME, HIS WAY

"Can this happen for me?" I imagine you're asking. Yes, it can. But it won't happen immediately. We'd like to magically heal with a quick reading of this book, but because God is invested in lasting change, He's chosen to use time and other people to accomplish healing in our lives.

It takes time and reflection to recognize the lies we've believed and the wounds we've amassed in our sexual pasts. We also need time to process how our pasts have wounded us and to reprogram negative thought patterns and destructive behaviors. Time allows our pain to heal so that oxytocin can be produced and released again. It takes time to break down walls, to risk being authentic and open, and to build emotional intimacy with your husband. It didn't happen overnight for me, or for the women whose stories you've read in this book. And it probably won't happen overnight for you.

But be encouraged. You have already begun to heal. The steps in this book have given you a great beginning. You've identified your wounds, addressed them and the lies you've believed, broken the bonds formed in your past, and begun the hard work of building emotional intimacy with your husband. You've made yourself accessible for God to do His healing work in you. Don't be discouraged if you don't feel instantly healed or dramatically interested in sex. God's ways are perfect. His plans for us unparalleled. He will heal you at your pace, in His time, and in His way.

A MUST-READ

As He heals, God will use His Word. God's book on sex, the Song of Songs, as it's titled in the New International Version of the Bible, is a must read for everyone desiring to reignite sexual passion in marriage. You'll find this tiny book tucked between Ecclesiastes (right next to Proverbs) and Isaiah. Written by King Solomon, it's a book that theologians believe describes the meeting, courtship, engagement, and marriage between King Solomon and his wife. Although King Solomon inherited many wives from his father David and went on to acquire many more (against God's will), this book attests to the exclusive love and relationship he had with this wife.

Don't let Solomon's many wives hinder you from discovering the truths in this book. Throughout history God used sinful, broken people to share His message. Remember, these aren't Solomon's words, they're God's. This is His truth, inspired by Him through Solomon's pen. Regardless of how you feel about Solomon, this book expresses the pure, beautiful love God intends for marriage—emotionally and physically. And quite possibly His unconditional, unfailing love for us.

A small book—only eight chapters—Song of Songs is best understood when read entirely at one sitting. But reading it once won't be enough. The way to let this book seep into your heart and change your view of sex is to read it multiple times over the next several weeks. It's written as poetry, with various code words from the cultural times to describe marital love. These words and phrases won't be familiar to you, and so this book may confuse you the first few times you read it. Stick with it. I did, and with each reading God gave me greater understanding, letting the concepts speak directly to my situation. He'll do that for you too.

As my husband and I went through our fast from sex, I read Song of Songs every day for five days in a row. With each reading I'd pray and ask God to show me what He wanted me to see. The first time, I only understood one concept from the book. As I faithfully read, God opened my eyes to digest His truth. He showed me lies I'd believed about sex and how those lies had kept me from experiencing His design for sex. The truth I was learning set me free—and set our sexual relationship free.

So the exercise I have for you in this chapter is this: over the next couple weeks, read Song of Songs at least five to seven times. The more the better. I still read it once in a while, and God continues to show me more. As you read, use a study Bible that offers a commentary or explanation of various words, phrases, and concepts in the book. My favorite translations are the New International Version (NIV) and the New American Standard (NASB). Both offer study Bible editions that I wouldn't be without.

I think you'll find it helpful to also read a few of the many books on the market that offer a layman's perspective on Song of Songs. My favorite is *Intimacy Ignited* by Joseph and Linda Dillow and Peter and Lorraine Pintus. They take you chapter by chapter through Song of Songs, helping you apply its truths to your marriage.

Before you begin this exercise, pray and ask God to open your mind to understand what He wants to say to you through this book. Ask that His Holy Spirit teach you and help you apply what you're reading to your own life. After each reading of the entire book of Song of Songs, ask yourself the following questions. You can jot down your answers below or in a separate notebook.

1. What words, phrases, verses, or concepts stood out for you as you read through Song of Songs? List them here.

_____

_____

_____

_____

_____

_____

_____

_____

2. How did God apply anything from your list to you personally?
   to your marriage?

_____

_____

_____

_____

_____

_____

3. What lie about sex, yourself, your husband, or God did God
   reveal in this reading?

_____

_____

_____

_____

_____

_____

_____

_____

4. What new truth has He shown you?

_____

_____

_____

_____

_____

_____

_____

5. How does He want you to apply what you've learned to your marriage?

_____

_____

_____

_____

_____

_____

Don't be discouraged if your first reading leaves you scratching your head. Keep an open mind. I find that the people who fail to glean any truth from Song of Songs are those who decide in advance they have nothing to receive. God promises that when we seek Him with all our hearts, we will find him. He loves that you're willing to seek Him in His Word. Faithfully persevere. He will not disappoint you. Just when you think there's no more to learn, He'll flood you with so much, you'll burst trying to take it all in.

FROSTING ON THE CAKE

Remember, you can't reignite desire without first building emotional intimacy. Learning to trust your husband again. Taking time to heal past and present hurts. Healing in the present involves discovering God's design for sex, love, and intimacy in marriage. Of course there are some great books on how to make sex more enjoyable for you and your husband. We'll get to those later, in chapter 12. Then, as your emotional intimacy grows, the how-to of great sex will be the frosting on the cake.

Pass the Healing On

When we allow God to heal our pasts, our choices flow like a stream of living water through us to bless our husbands and children with newfound hope and truth. Healing breaks the destructive cycle of generational sin, such as abuse and promiscuity, addictions, and pornography. It gives us confidence and strength to guide our children in what we know is right, despite opposition. No longer self-absorbed with our pain, we can focus on others' needs. But most importantly, healing gives us back our voice. No longer silenced by a muzzle of pain and shame, we can now speak positively into the lives of others.

What a miracle—that God would take the mess of our lives, and through healing turn them into messages of truth and hope for others! There's rarely a day that goes by that I don't thank God for what He's done in me. And for His grace in using my story to encourage others to find healing. Healing changes us in positive ways we can't hide. Others will notice and be changed by it too, particularly when we as parents, leaders, and friends give voice to the healing God has created in our lives and hearts.

AS A PARENT

Martha knows this firsthand. She came to me in despair. She'd been married and divorced three times, and was living with a man who was on his way to being husband number four. Her life was out of control, and she was lost. She'd recently given her life to God, and He'd already spoken to her about moving out of her boyfriend's house. I applauded her for surrendering her past, present, and future to God.

As she went through our study, God showed her many things: why she kept picking men who were harmful for her, why she feared commitment, and how staying bonded to past lovers had inhibited complete oneness in her previous marriages. As she grew, she began to share with her oldest daughter what God was teaching her. At twenty-one, her daughter was living with her boyfriend, getting ready to marry him. She had followed her mother's habitual pattern well. In the past, Martha had disapproved of her daughter's choices and told her so. But her hypocritical words fell on deaf ears, because she herself didn't live according to them.

That changed when Martha allowed God to heal her. From this new place of grace and truth, she began to touch her daughter's life. Rather than feeling judged, her daughter saw a new strength and joy in her mother. With actions behind them, these new words made sense. As a result, her daughter decided to move out of her boyfriend's house, go back to church, and stop having sex until marriage. I can still hear the astonishment in Martha's voice when she shared this news with me.

Martha later met a wonderful Christian man with whom she built a solid relationship without having sex prior to marriage. When I met her recently, she glowed with the blessing of having found the loving relationship she's always longed for but could never achieve on her own.

The impact of her healing continues, positively influencing her younger daughters who are still living at home. Not only is Martha now able to speak truth to her daughters about love, sex, and marriage, but her actions provide a healthy model of how to build a relationship God's way.

While you can't change the choices you made in the past, because of healing you can influence the choices your children make in the future. Your newfound voice of truth will ring loud and strong, backed by your life to prove it. Sure, there are no guarantees your children won't make some mistakes of their own. That's life, after all. But the changes your kids observe in you make it more likely that your words of grace and truth will be heeded.

One of the ways to use your voice as a parent is to tell your kids your story, when and if God leads you to do so. He knows your family best, so pray and ask Him guide you in this decision, and then wait. Wait until you've had healing so that your story is about what God has done in you, rather than a story told out of shame or a personal need to come clean. And wait until your children are old enough to absorb what you have to say.

Some parents are concerned that telling their kids about their past sins and mistakes will give their children license to do the same. I don't know if that is the case. As I get to know God better, I realize that everything about Him is truth and honesty. I believe that in most cases He will lead you to be open with your family. If your children are still young, wait until they're beginning to ask questions about sex, and use your story as a teachable moment for them.

In my case three of our children were older, in their early twenties, when I went through healing and God led me to share with them. But I sensed that our youngest son, in his teens, wasn't yet ready to hear my whole story. And so I waited two more years to tell him. God confirmed when it was the right time. He will do the same for you. Wait on Him for the right opportunity. Then you'll know that your children are in a healthy place to receive what you have to share.

You may also be wondering how much to tell your kids. When I told my children about my sexual past, I didn't go into detail about how many sexual partners I had, who they were, or any graphic details. Nor did I go into detail about the abortion. I answered their questions, but I kept to generalities rather than specifics. I recommend that you do the same. Your kids may want more details, but let them know that the details aren't necessary or relevant. The important part of your story is what God has done to restore you.

Another way to use your voice is to protect your children from sexual predators and abusers, particularly if you've received healing for childhood sexual abuse. I'm alarmed by the number of sexually abused women whose mothers were also abused as children. Even more alarming is that when these daughters told their mothers of the abuse, they were ignored or, worse, blamed. If you've gone through healing, God will help you break this damaging cycle, making you far less likely to be unaware when your kids are in a potentially dangerous situation or to ignore your child's cry for help. You've dealt with your own pain, so you can address what's going on with your kids.

Use your voice to warn your children against sexual predators. Teach young children not to expose their private parts to anyone or to let anyone touch them inappropriately. Ingrain in them the need to share with you if the behavior or communication of anyone (family member, friend, stranger) makes them feel uncomfortable or unsafe in any way. Sexual predators often threaten harm if their victims tell anyone what is going on, or they tell children that what happened is their fault, instilling shame. Prepare your children for these lies and let them know they can safely come to you, regardless of what they've been told by anyone else.

Healing gives us back our courage. Opens our eyes to the truth. Frees us from our own prison so we are able to release those we love from theirs. Enables us to confront the danger with boldness and truth, and remove our children from harm's way.

In addition, you can use your voice to talk to your kids about the following:

- God's design for marriage, between one man and one woman (see Genesis 2:24).
- God's command to keep sex inside marriage and why (see Hebrews 13:4; 1 Corinthians 6:18–20). God's command is not to spoil our fun, but to save us from the wounds caused by sex, and the bonds we form that will harm our marriage one day. Talk to your teens about the brain and sex and how God designed us to bond to every person we have sex with. And how we bring each past partner with us into marriage, inhibiting our ability to have the kind of bond we want in marriage.
- What constitutes sex. Teach your kids that it doesn't just mean having intercourse. It also includes oral and anal sex, mutual masturbation—any sexual expression that leads to arousal and release belongs inside marriage.
- How sex progresses. We often tell our children not to have sex but then neglect to inform them that sex is a natural progression and that arousal prepares their bodies to have sex. They need to be informed how this progression happens and what to do to avoid arousal if they want to abstain from sex. The natural progression moves from hand holding to hugging, to the simple

kiss, to the prolonged kiss, and finally the French kiss. French kissing generally causes the male to be aroused. Once aroused he will proceed to petting (touching with the hand or mouth under the clothes), which is generally when the female gets aroused. At this point, unless someone stops or they're interrupted, two aroused people will likely progress to sexual intercourse. Arousal points vary per individual, so assessing both partners' arousal triggers and setting a boundary to avoid them will ensure that neither partner will progress to sexual release.

- Why it's important to abstain from sex until marriage. Teach them that sex outside marriage is not the same as sex inside marriage and can ruin sexual intimacy inside marriage. God designed sex in marriage to enhance a foundation of friendship and emotional intimacy that's already been established. Sex outside marriage is often motivated by selfish desire, is hurried, usually in secret, and associated with fear of pregnancy and STDs. The majority of women I talk to who had sex outside marriage regret it, feel used, and carry the shame and guilt into their adult lives, where it undermines their desire and enjoyment of sex in marriage.

- Warn your children against the danger of pornography. Tell them it is addictive, and explain how bonding to it will inhibit their ability to be aroused by their spouse one day. Put safeguards on your television and computer so your children aren't exposed to sexually explicit material.

- Guard your boys from sexually aggressive girls, especially older ones, and don't allow your girls to date older boys. Let your children know it's okay to say no to sex. Warn them against alcohol and drugs, as they often lead to sexual activities your children weren't planning on participating in or are forced into.

- Warn your girls that when they dress in revealing clothing or in a sexual manner, they attract boys who are interested in sex.
- Above all, assure your children that you love them, believe in them, have hope for their future, and are there for them, no matter what happens. Start early, look for teachable moments, and initiate the conversations. In all of this you'll be building a relationship with them that allows for openness between you and assures your children that you are a safe person to talk with.

Visit my Web site, www.barbarawilson.org, for a list of resources that can help you prepare your children for their future as sexual beings.

AS A LEADER

Unfortunately, in many churches and ministries, leaders are not providing a safe, accepting environment in which people are free to deal with the shameful secrets.

For twenty years I attended a church where no one talked about their pasts. I assumed everyone else was perfect and I was the only one who'd messed up. Then unexpectedly God brought us to another church when my husband's job required us to move. At the new church, the women's pastor was strategic about making her ministry a safe place for women to heal from all kinds of issues. I had no idea what God was bringing me to as I began to hear women share their testimonies of abortion, abuse, eating disorders, and promiscuity. What I heard intrigued and scared me at the same time. As I listened to other women talking about the healing and victory they'd experienced, and as I watched them being accepted by everyone without judgment, I felt encouraged to surrender my secret shame to God.

Although Rachel, our pastor of women's ministry, had a squeaky-clean past, God had laid it on her heart to reach out with love, grace, and acceptance to those who didn't. I remember the fear I felt when I told her about my abortion and the healing journey God was taking me on. She came over to where I was sitting and, with tear-filled eyes, put her arm around me and prayed for me. I was afraid she'd reject me and banish me from serving. But instead she expressed joy at my obedience and the miracle God was doing in me. Since then she's been instrumental in opening doors in support of the ministry God has called me to. For me, the best part is that our friendship never changed. Even though we had moved because of my husband's job, I believe that God was the One who moved us because He had a purpose in mind—to heal me. I'm so grateful He did.

If you're a leader who is going through healing for your sexual past, you are in a position to help many others in your ministry. If you are like me, you might be hesitant to tell others about your past, afraid you'll never serve again. But as you step out in courage to talk about what God is doing in you, He will replace your shame with praise, allowing you the freedom to be authentic with others. As frightening as this step is, I've discovered that authentic ministries start with authentic leaders who share from a place of healing and hope. When we tell our stories from a place of shame, the stories are about us. But when we tell our stories from a place of healing, they are about God and what He's done. When others see that we've struggled but found healing, they find courage to trust God with their secrets too. If we become honest and open about the issues we have struggled with, our ministries will explode. Why? Because people are looking for a place to address life's hurts without fear of judgment. When the church provides such a place, people flock in.

Pray and ask God how you can make your ministry, from the smallest to the largest, a safe place for people to find healing. Don't wait for someone else to start; let God begin with you. As you find healing, tell others how God has broken the invisible bonds that kept you tied to your past and how this has impacted your marriage for the better. If you don't have a sexual past but, like my friend Rachel, you are aware that many women in your ministry do, you can help them by sharing your platform with women who recount the miracle of Jesus's rescuing work in their lives. This is what Rachel is doing. And the result? Streams of living water are flowing from our women. *And people are flocking in.*

AS A FRIEND

Most of the women who call me and ask to join my sexual healing Bible study do so because a friend shared her journey with them and encouraged them to find healing themselves. When we as women find sexual healing, it unleashes a new voice in us, a voice of hope instead of despair, joy instead of mourning.

Authentic people are contagious. Like magnets we draw others close with our honesty and grace. God uses us to impact others, one by one. Maybe you've noticed that happening already. As God is changing you and your marriage, perhaps you are opening up with others. In response, they're baring their secrets to you. Out of this new place of hope, you're able to encourage them to say yes to God and surrender their past to Him.

In chapter 1 I shared an excerpt from the testimony Arlene gave at her weekly MOPs (Mothers of Preschoolers) group, where she was a leader. What God has done in the lives of the women who heard Arlene's testimony is beyond what any of us could have imagined. All because one woman said yes to God and surrendered her past to Him.

In just a few weeks, Arlene will be starting our first sexual healing Bible study exclusively for MOPs moms. It was never her plan to start a movement when God nudged her to trust Him with her past. It was never mine, either. But it was God's. As a transparent leader and friend, Arlene has influenced an entire ministry, from the leadership down. You may be thinking that you could tell your story to one other person, but that you'd panic at the thought of speaking to a crowd. Don't worry. God may not ask that of you. And if He does—whether it's to five people or one hundred—He'll give you the words to say and the strength to utter them. Remember that your healing isn't just about you. God, a master at multitasking, loves to duplicate in others what He's done for us. You'll be overwhelmed with joy when He uses you in someone else's life. It's a calling you can't resist. So be willing. Trust God to bring those He's nudging into your path. Trust Him to give you everything you need as you partner with Him in another's healing journey.

You might have noticed that this message is different from the one I gave you in chapter 6. There I cautioned you to pray before you told your story to others. Prior to complete healing, your wounds make you vulnerable and you need to take care you aren't wounded again by another's callous response. But healing changes that. Once you've been healed, you're able to separate yourself from your past. You no longer identify yourself with what you've done. Instead you see what God's done in you. If others reject you now, there's less of an impact. Shame no longer controls you or dictates your feeling of self-worth. Others' views of you take a backseat to God's view. Instead of rejecting you, they're rejecting what

God has done in you. That's often more about their fear of what God is convicting in them than it is about you or your story.

Although God will use you in the lives of your married friends, His message of healing is for everyone. The world's view of sex has wounded us all, married or not, and the steps to healing and breaking past bonds are universal. Here are some thoughts to help you as you support others in their healing journey:

- *Listen to their stories without judgment.* Offer others grace, love, acceptance, and hope. Refrain from negative comments such as "You should have," "Why didn't you?" or "How could you?" Do not respond with shock or disgust. Be gentle and compassionate. Those who experience grace and acceptance in response to their stories will be encouraged to tell others as they pursue healing.

- *Keep eye contact.* Shame often compels us to lower our eyes. Look each person in the eye. When others are assured of your loving response, they are encouraged to continue their story. In certain situations, appropriate physical touch—a hand on a shoulder or arm—can provide comfort and acceptance as well.

- *Give others this book if they're married, or* The Invisible Bond: How to Break Free from Your Sexual Past *if they're single.* A resource that speaks to their situation will give them hope and direction as they discover God's steps of healing.

- *Through prayer, help them discern their next step.* Are they in danger of physical harm? Ensure that they take immediate steps to protect themselves and their children. Would counseling help? Would they benefit from joining a support or recovery group for their particular need? Research available resources for them. Offer to accompany them the first time they go to a group or counseling, if that would be helpful.

- *Offer to be a support to them as they go through healing, praying for them and helping them process what God is showing them.*
- *If they reject all that you have to offer, love them anyway.* Trust God with them. He's the One working in them, and His timing is always best.

PERFECTION NOT REQUIRED

We don't have to be perfect or to have it all figured out for God to use us. One of God's most effective strategies is to use broken people to speak truth into others' lives. Many of the men and women God used in the Bible to change history sinned and made plenty of mistakes, just like us. There are even some with sexual pasts. In fact, of the five women in the genealogy of Christ, three had sexual pasts: Tamar seduced her father-in-law (see Genesis 38); Rahab was once a prostitute (see Joshua 2; 6; Matthew 1:5); and Bathsheba committed adultery with King David (see 2 Samuel 11–12). So don't be surprised if God begins to use you long before you feel ready.

Remember, God can redeem *anything*—your worst sin, your greatest shame, your deepest pain—whatever it is. God not only forgives and heals everything but then also uses you for His purpose in ways you can't imagine. Most wives have sex before marriage, which means women you know in your family, your church, and your neighborhood may be struggling with sex too. They don't know that God has the hope they're seeking, the answers to all their questions. Until now, there's been no one to tell them. No one to show them the way.

But not anymore, because now...*they have you.*

Common Questions,
Helpful Answers

Everyone's story is different, and we each have different needs and questions. For that reason you may have questions this book has not answered. In this chapter I'll address some of the questions I've received over the years. Maybe you'll find your own questions here. If not, you'll be prepared with answers to offer others when similar questions arise. If your question isn't addressed here, I invite you to go to my Web site, barbarawilson.org, click on Contact Us, and send me an e-mail.

I'm a widow, and I recently remarried. Do I need to break the bond with my deceased spouse?

When we create bonds God's way, within marriage, they are positive, healthy bonds and will have no negative impact on a future relationship. However, if your husband was abusive or if you had sex prior to marriage, then you need to break the bond, because it could weaken intimacy in your current marriage. If you are not sure, pray and ask God if there's a negative bond from your previous marriage that you need to sever and heal from. God knows best, and He'll be sure to show you.

I'm divorced and remarried. Do I need to break the bond with my ex-husband?

Divorce tears apart two people who have become one—emotionally, physically, and spiritually. That never happens without significant pain and wounding. Unlike the bond mentioned in the first question, the bond with an ex-husband needs to be broken because of the negative emotions associated with it that will be a burden in your new marriage. Although you may not be able to physically remove this person from your life, especially if children are involved, it will be important to ask God to sever the "one flesh" bond you had with him so that you can completely bond with your present husband.

How do I know if what I experienced is sexual abuse?

Great question. Sexual abuse can take many forms. We often think of sexual abuse in terms of intercourse. Although sexual abuse is often associated with sexual touching and intercourse, you can be abused without even being touched. Dr. Dan Allender, in *The Wounded Heart: Hope for Adult Victims of Childhood Sexual Abuse*, defined sexual abuse as "any contact or interaction (visual, verbal, psychological) between a child/adolescent and an adult when the child/adolescent is being used for the sexual stimulation of the perpetrator or any other person."[1] He goes on to describe two categories of sexual abuse: sexual contact and sexual interactions. "Sexual contact involves any type of physical touch that is designed to arouse sexual desire (physical or psychological) in the victim and/or the perpetrator."[2] Physical touch can be forced or non-forced and progress from kissing to sexual touch of clothed or unclothed body parts to genital stimulation and penetration.

Sexual interactions are harder to define and easier for the victim to minimize. Examples include

- being exposed to sexually arousing stimuli by an older adolescent or adult,
- sexual conversation that leaves a child feeling uncomfortable and violated, and
- having your body scrutinized by adults who violate your privacy when dressing or showering, and/or by using sexually explicit language to describe body parts.

More subtle forms of abuse are psychological in nature. An example is a care-giving adult who parades around the home naked or involves a child as a surrogate or confidante in a sexually subtle way to the exclusion of the other spouse. Regardless of the kind or severity of sexual abuse, all forms wound us and cause us shame.

An abuser can be anyone: a father, grandfather, brother, family friend or relative, baby-sitter, stepparent, pastor, or a mother's boyfriend. Although females are more often abused by males, they can also be abused by other females. The abuser can be any age—even the same age as the victim. If you're still wondering if you've been abused, ask God to reveal any memory or situation in which you felt sexually uncomfortable, awkward, or violated. Don't be afraid if something comes to mind, and don't try to minimize it or deny it happened. Trust that God has revealed it so you can find healing and be free from the damaging wounds of this abuse. Share your abuse with your husband, a Christian counselor, a pastor, or a trusted friend, and let God begin the journey of setting you free.

Some women tell me that they sense they were abused as a child but have no specific memories to validate their suspicions. If this is your experience, you may want to see a counselor to help you recall events as you go through healing. But if memories aren't forthcoming, trust that God has chosen not to reveal the specifics to you at this time and that for whatever reason, it's not necessary for your healing right now. If indeed you were abused, God will make it known to you if and when it's necessary.

Even though I've gone through healing and want to improve our sex life, my husband seems to have lost interest in me sexually. Is there anything I can do?

Although your husband may appear to have lost interest in you, the reality may be that he is hesitant to pursue you sexually because you've made a habit of avoiding or rejecting his intimate advances in the past. A man's sense of manhood, his feeling of self-worth, is closely tied to his sexuality. When we desire our husbands, respond to their touch, we make them feel loved and give them strength. We give them the courage to rise up on our behalf, to be our knights who love and protect us. But each rejection, like a knife, pierces their confidence and sense of worth, until they're too wounded to keep pursuing.

This was true for Stacey's husband, even though her attitude toward sex and her husband was changing. She was open to sex, hoping, waiting for him to pursue her because, although she was ready, she was still afraid. She needed her husband to help her through this, to make it safe for her. But he was afraid too. Her previous rejections had left a wound that time had yet to heal. And so he waited for her to come to him. But the pressure to pursue paralyzed Stacey. Sex was still a fragile thing for her. Being responsive would prove challenging enough; having to pursue was beyond her reach.

Maybe this is your story, and now you and your husband are more like roommates than soul mates. Pray and ask God to show you the wounds you've caused your husband by rejecting him for so long. Then ask your husband how it feels when you say no to sex, over and over. Maybe his anger, indifference, or absence is more about feeling unloved than about being in a bad mood. Or maybe feeling unloved is what's behind his being overly critical, demanding, and unkind. I'm not saying that these behaviors are acceptable. I just know that when I don't feel loved or appreciated, I can become like this.

Knowing the health of Stacey's marriage and the support her husband was giving her in this healing journey, I suggested that they reverse the roles. I recommended that she give her husband permission to pursue her sexually, with the promise that she would respond willingly and not reject him. And I suggested a reasonable goal of two times a week. Stacey was relieved at this arrangement, and her husband agreed. When I asked her recently how things were going, she said much better, though they have more work to do. Healing wounds, restoring intimacy, and reversing old patterns take time.

You may want to suggest a similar arrangement to your husband if he has stopped pursuing you. But I'll offer one caution: I hesitate to suggest this if your husband would use it to his advantage rather than as an opportunity to help you heal. Keep in mind that your husband may have lost interest in you sexually for another reason. Possible reasons include:

- He's had sexual abuse in his past.
- His levels of testosterone are low.

- He's being unfaithful.
- He's addicted to pornography.

Pray that God will give you insight into the reason. Ask your husband about what is impacting his desire for sex with you. If you discern that it is due to your previous rejections, talk together to set a maximum number of times a week that would be comfortable for you, with the understanding that anything beyond that you have permission to refuse. Knowing up-front what you're comfortable with will minimize his feelings of rejection. It's a win-win arrangement. The pressure for both of you is gone; he's happier, you're gradually healing, and the sex is bonding you closer and closer. Before long you may forget about your limit altogether.

My husband reconnected with his high school sweetheart during his high school reunion. Now he's e-mailing her all the time. Is this something I should worry about?

Yes! This is a definite cause for concern. If a couple's bond is not what it should be because of past bonds, a spouse with an invisible bond to a previous partner will be easily tempted to fantasize about a past relationship or to become involved in emotional or physical affairs. Spouses who gravitate toward someone in their past are often having struggles in their marriages.

Your husband needs to break this bond with his high school sweetheart. It has prevented him from forming an emotional attachment to you, and it's why he is easily drawn to the past. He may not realize that his attachment to the past has to do with the bond he created. But there is hope. If he's willing to seek healing and to break the bonds to the past, you will be able to rebond in your marriage with the complete oneness God intended.

If self-stimulation is in my past, have I created a bond that needs to be broken?

It depends on whether you used mental or visual images during self-stimulation. If mental or visual images were involved, you may have trained your brain to be aroused by certain stimuli, in which case you may be struggling to enjoy sex in the absence of those images. If this is your situation, it would explain why, even though you're having sex with your husband, you may need to conjure up those past mental images to get aroused. It may also explain why, although you're happily married, you're still struggling with self-stimulation. In addition to asking God to sever this bond, you'll need to take steps to retrain your brain's arousal trigger.

Here are several steps to consider:

- Confess your struggle to your husband.
- Get professional counseling.
- Practice taking every thought captive (see 2 Corinthians 10:3–5).
- Join a Celebrate Recovery group at your church that offers support for addictions to sex or pornography.
- Pray before and during sex with your husband that God will protect your thoughts and keep them pure.
- Guard your eyes, ears, and mind from sexually explicit material.

My husband has a bad temper, and he often lashes out at me. Sometimes he says horrible things to me. He always apologizes afterward, but it makes it hard for me to trust him or want to have sex with him. What can I do?

A person's anger or pain *never* excuses verbally abusive behavior. Verbal attacks, rage, and belittling are never okay in a marriage relationship.

If your husband is verbally or emotionally abusive to you, consider seeking professional help. A professional counselor can help you learn how to respond to his attacks in an emotionally healthy way. If your husband is willing to go with you, a counselor can help him uncover the root of his anger and learn how to express it in healthy and appropriate ways. If you're unsure that what you're experiencing is abuse, talk with someone you trust, or with a Christian counselor, for guidance.

However, if your husband is physically abusing you or your children, your first responsibility is to protect yourself and your children. *It's crucial for all concerned that you remove yourself and your kids from a physically abusive relationship.* Counseling could help your husband stop being abusive, but that won't happen as long as you stay and bear the abuse in silence. Your relationship won't heal because, as long as you are in an abusive situation, you'll never feel safe enough to risk emotional intimacy. Nor will you heal.

I understand if you're scared. Leaving the security of a marriage is never easy. Planning how you'll raise and support your family can seem like an ominous task. But you're not alone. God has a special place in His heart for the fatherless and the widow, or the wife whose husband does not honor his commitment to love and protect her. God is the true source of your provision and protection, not your husband. As you leave to protect yourself and your children, God goes with you and promises to *never* leave you. He will guide you to safety. He will provide for all your needs, emotionally, physically, and spiritually. He will love you completely, unconditionally, like no man ever can. You can trust Him—I promise.

I have a history of emotional and physical affairs. If I break the bonds I've created, does that mean I won't be tempted again in the future? If not, what can I do to guard my heart and my marriage?

Breaking past bonds and healing wounds allows you to restore emotional and physical intimacy with your husband, leaving you less vulnerable to attachments to other men. As you continue to draw closer to your husband, you will most likely find that you no longer struggle with the need for attention from other men. However, if this has been your weakness in the past, it can be again in the future if you allow your emotional relationship with your husband to suffer. Carefully read the suggestions offered in the next chapter about how to keep your relationship strong and your healing moving forward.

Close Today, Closer Tomorrow

Marriage takes work. And people aren't perfect. Even with healing we will still have challenges being on the same page sexually with our husbands. But that's okay. That's where love, patience, and forgiveness shine best. And as we struggle through our differences, our intimacy grows and matures.

Some of you may be asking, "How do I know if I've had healing?" You're still struggling, and even though you have gone through the steps in the book, you still don't enjoy sex. Others of you may be asking, "How can I make it last?" You are singing a new song, especially in the area of sex. You have newfound desire for your husband but are afraid things will go back to where they were before. Both are great questions—ones I'll attempt to answer in this chapter.

How Do I Know If I've Had Healing?

If you've gone through the steps in this book and are still struggling to feel desire, don't despair. Regardless of where you're at in the area of sexual desire, you are healing. How do I know? *Because it's not possible to grow closer to God and remain the same.* As He permeates our hearts and minds with the light of His truth, we can't help but change. But often it's so gradual, we don't notice.

If you are still struggling, pray and ask God to show you if you need healing in additional areas. Remember, healing is a journey. It takes time. God reveals things one at a time, as we can handle them. Trust that this is His perfect pace for you.

If God reveals to you other areas in which you need healing, talk with a Christian counselor, pastor, or trusted friend. When someone objective speaks into your situation, it can help you find that missing piece. Don't be afraid to ask God to heal you completely, even your desire for sex. So often we get caught up in the steps and forget to simply ask. God wants to heal us, but often He doesn't get the opportunity because we don't ask.

When you ask, expect to be surprised. God answers in ways we seldom foresee. Although you'd like to wake up one day with a surge of sexual desire, it probably won't happen that way. Instead, as you trust and follow His leading, the answer will likely sneak up on you unaware. How so? Because as you get to know God better, the awe of Him will overshadow your initial request. There'll be so many other delights along the way to knowing Him that He will become your focus, instead of your quest for sexual healing.

One way to measure your healing is by redoing some of the exercises in chapter 5—the inventory of symptoms and problems, the evaluation of the impact of your past on your present, and your current view of sex—and comparing how you felt then to how you feel now. You'll be amazed, I promise. Even if you're not as far along as you want to be, you'll be encouraged by how far you've come.

That's what happened to me after I went through a Bible study that focused on healing for abortion. Prior to my healing I filled out a symptom checklist similar to the one you did in chapter 5. I was surprised when I rated many of the items with 2s and 3s, or moderate to intense. Throughout the study I knew God was healing me; I could feel it. But I had no idea how much until I filled out the same checklist at the end. All my 2s and 3s had become 0s and 1s. As I got closer to God, His presence in my life was slowly changing me, except I hadn't noticed just how much until I compared my before and after lists. I was too focused on Him and our amazing relationship to consider what was happening to me.

If you've had some healing, and your desire has returned, you may be wondering if the healing will last. If so, I want to prepare you for what to expect in the future.

How Can I Make It Last?

As you've worked through this book, you may have received significant healing already. You feel brand-new. Your marriage has never been better. God's given you a new sex life—better than you'd ever imagined. If so, I'm overjoyed for you. Treasure this time. Let it bond you and your husband closer as you continue to heal. But don't be surprised or discouraged if it doesn't always feel this way.

For the past four years I've lived free from the emotional and sexual baggage that had dampened my view of sex for all those years. And the result has been a deepening love and intimacy with my husband. A closeness I could never have imagined. A love and desire for him beyond what I could have achieved on my own—only through what God has done in me. And a desire and enjoyment of sex I never knew possible.

But does that mean I'm always ready for sex? always in the mood? Unfortunately no. Age, health, fatigue, pressures, busyness, and worries can each threaten my willingness and readiness for sex. But that doesn't mean the healing wasn't real or that it won't last.

The work God does in our lives will last for all eternity. No one, nothing, can snatch His gift from us. The wounds He's healed will always be healed. The lies He's replaced with His truth will never deceive us again. The bonds to past partners He's severed are powerless over us now. That work is done, finished.

However, that doesn't mean our level of desire will always remain what it is now. A woman's sexual desire ebbs and flows with external and internal influences. While most healthy men always desire and want sex, this isn't so for women. Many variables affect our desire for sex, including those listed here.

- *Hormonal fluctuations.* Our desire can change from week to week to correspond with our menstrual cycle. Then there are the hormonal changes that happen during and after pregnancy. Even more significant are the hormonal changes that happen as we head into menopause, when levels of estrogen, progesterone, and testosterone all take a dive, impacting desire. Mood and desire can also fluctuate with the use of hormone replacements and birth control.

- *The busyness of life.* As multitaskers, women juggle many roles—mother, wife, employee, daughter, and friend, for example. Our responsibilities can squeeze every moment of our time, leaving little opportunity to "get in the mood" for romance. Certain times in our lives are busier than others, especially when the children are young. The more we're stretched, the greater our fatigue and the less we desire sex.

- *Prescription medication.* Sleeping pills, antidepressants, and antianxiety and pain medications can all diminish desire.
- *Health.* Illness, especially chronic pain or fatigue, can also steal desire.
- *Emotions.* The myriad of emotions we experience as women every day can impact sexual desire. If we're hurt, angry, sad, or frustrated, setting our emotions aside in order to enjoy sex can take some effort.
- *Stress.* As the greatest thief of our ability to enjoy life, stress robs us of many things, including desire.

And of course we have an enemy, Satan, who'd love nothing more than to thrust a wedge into our intimacy and drive us apart.

I'm telling you this, not to discourage you, but to prepare you for these fluctuations and encourage you to continue moving forward in healing.

What helps my husband and me keep pressing forward, rather than retreating back to where we were? It's simple, yet so profound. I ask God to help me. I ask Him every day to keep my heart open, tender, willing. I ask Him to turn my heart toward my husband and give me love and desire for him that is beyond my human ability. I ask Him to give me a servant's heart toward my husband, to help me want to be there for him, even when I'm not in the mood. And when my body is there but my mind is somewhere else, I ask God to do what I can't do alone—change my attitude and focus my mind on this precious one He's given me to love. And I remember why God gave us sex. Not just for personal pleasure—because honestly sometimes I'd prefer sleep over pleasure. But for oneness, intimacy, connection, and comfort and to keep my husband's heart and mind turned on by me alone.

I asked some of the women I've counseled what advice they had to add about ways to keep the healing going for the long haul. Here are their ten ways:

1. *Keep your heart soft and open.* Keep praying that God will give you a tender, vulnerable, teachable heart, one that is more selfless than selfish, more forgiving than resentful, more open than closed, so that new hurts don't harden it.

2. *Take thoughts captive.* Instead of dwelling on the negative or nursing the hurts, give them to God and ask Him to comfort you. Ask Him to show you all of your spouse's good qualities so you don't focus on the negative.

3. *Stay close to God.* Trust God, not your husband, to meet all your needs and expectations. Release your husband from this impossible debt he'll never be able to pay.

4. *Remember sexually positive experiences with your husband.* Ask God to remind you so you'll be a willing recipient or the initiator the next time. As you focus on your husband sexually, your desire will increase. Pray that you'll respond to your husband's touch.

5. *Pray together.* The women I've counseled unanimously agreed that praying together is sexy. Why? Because it's so intimate. Nothing fosters desire in a woman more than feeling close emotionally.

6. *Turn off the TV.* Nothing sabotages great sex more.

7. *Make time to get away, just the two of you.* Just as it's easier to focus on God when we remove distractions, it's easier to focus on our spouses when we're not distracted. Have a weekly date. Go away for the weekend two or three times a year—or stay home, and let your kids go away. And if

finances allow, try to take an extended vacation once a year—even if it's for three to five days. Getting away occasionally saved my marriage. With four children, two of them with special needs, Eric and I had little time for each other. Even forty-eight hours away would remind us of why we fell in love in the first place and spark the romantic energy we needed to stay in the game.

8. *Read books together that help you grow in your marriage.* Read books that encourage communication. Some great resources include:

- *Intimate Encounters: A Practical Guide to Discovering the Secrets of a Really Great Marriage* by Dr. David and Teresa Ferguson and Dr. Chris and Holly Thurman is a wonderful book for facilitating discussions about emotional oneness that you might not normally have.

- *Intimacy Ignited: Conversations Couple to Couple* by Dr. Joseph and Linda Dillow and Dr. Peter and Lorraine Pintus will turn on your sex life as you study Song of Songs.

- *Moments with You: 365 All-New Devotions for Couples* by Dennis and Barbara Rainey offers 365 devotions with discussion and prayer tips to help you grow together spiritually.

- *Sheet Music: Uncovering the Secrets of Sexual Intimacy in Marriage* by Kevin Leman is a biblically based, how-to book on great sex.

- *Simply Romantic Nights* from FamilyLife helps bring a creative touch to your sex life. This resource kit includes cards for him and her with suggestions to help you plan and make your romantic moments memorable and lasting.

- *The Married Guy's Guide to Great Sex* by Clifford and Joyce Penner is a great book on God's design for sex.

9. *Have a vision for your future.* Together with your husband, make goals for your marriage: spiritual, physical, emotional, financial, and so on. Occasionally use your date night to review and evaluate how you're doing.

10. *Get counseling if you need it.* The wise counsel of a godly person can make all the difference in your marriage. It can offer a fresh perspective, help you see beyond yourself, and mediate struggles that have you stuck.

EXPECT GREAT THINGS

Wherever you are in your marriage, you have reason to hope. God is on your side, and He'll never give up on you or your husband. Philippians 1:6 says, "[Be] confident of this, that he who began a good work in you will carry it on to completion until the day of Christ Jesus." God began this good work in you, and He will carry it (and *you* and your marriage) on to completion—until Christ takes us home.

God is faithful. Faithful to His promise that if you trust Him with your past and with your marriage, He'll continue to heal you and your relationship, and draw you and your husband into the most intimate oneness you've ever known. He delights in pouring out His blessings on us, giving us good gifts. Gifts we don't deserve, haven't earned, and can never pay back. But we need to ask. We need to give up trying to do it on our own and ask the God of heaven, the Giver of good gifts to His children, to bless us, to bless our marriages. In Matthew 7:11 Jesus says, "If you, then, though you are evil, know how to give good gifts to your children, how much more will your Father in heaven give good gifts to those who ask him!"

You can't do it on your own. You can't fix yourself or your marriage. We're all good at getting into a mess on our own but are powerless to find our way out alone.

What do you long to ask God to do for your marriage? What good gift do you yearn for Him to unleash on you, on your marriage? Ask Him; pour out your heart to Him. Don't hold back. He wants to know. He longs to bless you with good things, with a great marriage. Do it right now. Right here. Start with, *Dear God, please help me…*

And once you've asked, once you've poured out your heart to Him, be willing to wait. Wait with expectation. With a restful, peaceful, trustful waiting founded on eager expectation that God will do what He's promised. And that He loves you enough to give you the best…His best. Because it's true. He does love you. And He is willing to give you His very best.

He's just waiting for you to ask.

Ten-Week Study Guide

You may choose to enhance the steps of healing in this book with this study guide. The combination of Scripture and application questions will give you an opportunity to draw closer to God on this healing journey.

You can go through the study alone and use what God is teaching you as discussion starters with your husband to encourage greater intimacy. Or you can do it with your husband. If he wants to join you, I recommend that you do the chapters on your own and then come together to discuss your answers. You can also use the book and study guide in a small-group setting with other wives. Confidentiality is essential in groups in which personal information is shared.

Week One
Read chapter 1, "Saying No When You Want to Say Yes."

1. What led you to read this book?
2. Of the different stories you read in chapter 1, which one do you relate to the most? Why? If not a story, what was something the author said that you related to?
3. What is your greatest struggle or regret in your marriage?
4. What are you hopeful God will do for you and your marriage through this healing journey?
5. Do you believe God can, will, and truly desires to heal you and your marriage? Why or why not?
6. Who is God *really?* Often we have a skewed view of Him because people and events in our past have caused us to see

God incorrectly. The following verses will help you discover truths about God: who He really is, how He feels about you, and what He says He will do for you.

Read the following verses and write down everything you learn about God.

- Exodus 34:6
- Deuteronomy 31:6
- Nehemiah 9:17
- Job 16:19–21
- Psalm 18:47
- Psalm 46:1, 7
- Isaiah 25:4
- Jeremiah 31:3–4
- Lamentations 3:22–25
- Joel 2:13
- 1 Peter 5:7
- 1 John 1:9
- 1 John 2:1–2

7. Describe God's love for you. Write down everything you learn from the following verses:
   - Psalm 103:8–17
   - John 3:16
   - Romans 5:5–8
   - Romans 8:35–39
   - Ephesians 3:16–21
   - 1 John 3:1
   - 1 John 4:8–11

8. What does God promise to do for you?
   - 2 Chronicles 7:14
   - Psalm 103:1–5
   - Isaiah 40:28–31
   - Isaiah 43:1–5
   - Isaiah 57:18–19
   - Isaiah 61:1–3
   - Jeremiah 33:3
   - Matthew 6:25–34
   - John 14:27
   - Romans 15:13
   - Philippians 4:6–7, 19

9. How have these verses changed your mind about who God is and how He feels about you?

10. How does knowing God better give you courage to trust Him to heal your sexual past, help you in your present marriage, and give you hope for the future?

We've just scratched the surface of learning who God really is, how much He loves us, and what He promises us. My prayer is that this Bible study will increase your desire to know more about God and want to have an intimate relationship with Him. After all, He sacrificed His life so that *He could have a relationship with you.*

Week Two
Read chapter 2, "The 'Superglue' Hormone."

1. Read Genesis 2:24; Matthew 19:5–6; and Mark 10:7–9, and answer these questions:

    a. Each of these scriptures starts with "For this reason." Read a verse or two before each one to find out what reason it is referring to. Why do you think God considers this so important that He mentions it more than once?

    b. Who makes the husband and wife "one flesh"? In comparison, who is responsible when a couple separates?

    c. Although a couple may separate, how does God still see them? How does this make you feel?

2. Read Malachi 2:15. In what ways does God make a husband and wife one?

3. Read 1 Corinthians 6:16. How is this verse similar to Genesis 2:24? A prostitute is someone who offers casual sex. According to this verse, what causes two people to become "one flesh"?

4. How does what you have learned about the brain and sex change your view of how God bonds us?

5. If, according to God, sex is the marriage and the breakup is the divorce, how many marriages and divorces have you experienced in your past?

6. How has becoming "one" with others in your past impacted you? your marriage?

7. Based on what you've learned, explain why it's necessary for the health of your marriage to break the bonds to past sexual partners.

8. Read Joel 2:25. If God could pay you back for everything you've lost, or had stolen from you because of your past, what would you ask Him for?

Week Three

Read chapter 3, "When Sex Doesn't Bring Pleasure."

1. Can you relate to the feelings of shame described at the beginning of chapter 3? If so, what is the source of your shame? What triggers shame for you?

2. Read 1 John 1:9 and James 5:16. What is the difference between forgiveness and healing? How does having healing help you feel God's forgiveness?

3. Read Psalm 34:5 and Isaiah 61:7. What does God want to replace your shame with?

4. Read Romans 8:1–2.
   a. If God doesn't condemn us, who is our condemner?
   b. Instead of living as condemned, how does God want us to live?
   c. How does living as though we're condemned cause us shame?

5. Read Hebrews 12:2. How did Jesus respond to shame?

6. Read Ephesians 5:25–27. Shame causes us to see ourselves as bad, dirty, stained. According to this passage, how does God really see us?

7. Whose story do you relate to in this chapter? Why?

8. If you and your husband had sex before marriage, how has that impacted how you see him now?

Week Four

Read chapter 4, "Emotionally Divided."

1. How did sex inhibit or replace emotional growth in your relationships before marriage?

2. If you had sex with your husband before marriage, what level of emotional intimacy had you reached when you began to have sex?

3. How has having sex at that time impacted your emotional and physical intimacy now?

4. Kissing is one of the most intimate forms of physical intimacy. Often it's harder to kiss than to have sex. Do you agree with this statement? Why or why not? If you tend to avoid kissing your husband, what do you think is at the root of your struggle?

5. How has the hooking-up culture impacted our ability to develop true emotional intimacy in relationships before and in marriage?

6. How have you denied your husband the opportunity to really know you intimately—before marriage and in your marriage now?

7. Read Psalm 139. How well does God know you? List all the ways this passage says He knows you.

8. Read Jeremiah 29:13–14. How can we know God? What does God promise when we seek Him wholeheartedly? How can we apply this to knowing our husbands?

Week Five

Read chapter 5, "Where Does It Hurt?"

If you're reading this book and doing the study in a small group, use this week to share your stories. Meet in a private place where there are no distractions. Remind everyone of the need for confidentiality.

Using the life map as a guide, share how your life has been impacted by sex from your earliest exposure to the present. Include a brief history of what's happened in your past, and how that's affected you today in your marriage. Make sure everyone has an equal amount of time to share by giving everyone a time limit and enlisting someone to keep track of each person's time. If time permits, you may use the questions below for further discussion. End your time with prayer and some hugs, making sure everyone leaves feeling loved and accepted.

If you're doing this on your own or with your husband, answer these questions after you've completed each exercise in this chapter:

1. What has God shown you about your past that is a new revelation for you?

2. After doing the exercises that address your current symptoms, what have you discovered about yourself?

3. How has your current view of sex been shaped by your past?

4. How have your sexual bonds from past relationships, or with your husband before marriage, affected your marriage?

5. Read Psalm 103:1–5. As you read each benefit God offers you, write out a specific prayer for what you'd like God to heal, redeem, and restore in you.

Week Six
Read chapter 6, "A Plan for Healing."

If you're doing this study in a small group, use this week to read some of your anger letters to each other as well as answer the questions below. If you're doing this study alone or with your husband, make sure you read your anger letters to your support person or your husband or both.

1. How has keeping secrets hurt you? your husband? your marriage?

2. Have you asked your husband to support you as you go through healing or to join you in reading this book? Why or why not? If so, how has he responded?

3. Do you have a support person as you go through this healing process? How has she been instrumental in your healing? Make sure you read your anger letters to her.

4. Looking at your list of those who have shared responsibility in your sexual wounding (see page 92), who do you feel the most anger toward? Do you have yourself and/or God on your list? Why or why not?

5. What losses are you grieving because of your past? (If you're doing this in a small group, together answer the questions on pages 98–99.)

6. What lies have deceived you because of your past? (If you're doing this in a small group, together answer the questions on pages 100–101.)

7. Read John 14:6 and John 8:31–32. Where do we find truth? What does knowing the truth do for us? Describe a truth that has set you free.

Week Seven

Read chapter 7, "Say Good-Bye to the Past."

1. How did you feel when you were writing your sexual history list? What did God show you that surprised or alarmed you about your list?

2. What did you experience as you prayed through your list? What has changed for you since praying through your list?

3. Read 2 Corinthians 7:10. Describe in your own words the difference between godly sorrow and worldly sorrow. How

have you experienced worldly sorrow for your past? Describe a time in this process when you felt godly sorrow.

4. Read Hebrews 12:1. How does this verse help you remove the tangible reminders of past relationships? How can these reminders hinder you from moving forward in your relationship with God and your husband?

5. Read 2 Corinthians 10:3–5. How can taking "captive every thought" and making it "obedient to Christ" fight the battle for your mind? What is so important about capturing our thoughts in the war against sin?

6. Read Matthew 18:21–35. Whom have you imprisoned because of unforgiveness? What repayment are you demanding from others because of your unforgiveness? What is the consequence for the servant who can't forgive? How have you imprisoned yourself because of unforgiveness?

Week Eight

Read chapter 8, "Become Your Husband's Best Friend."

1. Read Ezekiel 36:25–27. Does your heart sometimes feel like stone? What caused your heart to harden?

2. A "heart of flesh" is a broken heart, one that God can heal. Is God breaking your heart of stone? How so? If not, what is keeping it hardened? I encourage you to pray and ask God to break and soften your heart so you can heal.

3. Read James 4:6. What does God offer the woman who humbles herself? How does God respond to a proud heart? How are a hardened heart and a proud heart the same?

4. Read Hebrews 3:7–8. When does God say we harden our hearts? What is the response God desires?

5. Read Isaiah 66:2 and Psalm 34:18. What is God's response to those who are humble and broken?

6. Read Ephesians 2:14. Has there been a wall of hostility between you and your husband? How is God using your softened, humbled heart to help repair your marriage and build intimacy with your husband?

7. What does God need to change in *you* so your marriage can grow in the three ways mentioned in this chapter—spiritually, emotionally, and physically? Answer each one separately.

Week Nine

Read chapter 9, "It's Time to Be Lovers Again."

1. Of the six reasons God gave us sex, which one(s) are new for you? How does seeing sex from God's perspective change your view of it?

2. Which of the six purposes for sex have you experienced in your marriage? Which one(s) would you like to experience?

3. Read over your answers to the questions on pages 155–157. Summarize what God has been teaching you about sex as you read through Song of Songs.

4. As you review your answers on page 156, which lie(s) did God expose that has been the most destructive for you and your marriage?

5. What truths from Song of Songs has God been asking you to apply to your marriage?

6. What similarities are there between you and Solomon's wife? How are you different?

7. How is your husband similar to Solomon? How is he different?

8. This book describes what God intended for love and intimacy in marriage. If this is not your marriage right now, what hope does it give you that one day it can be?

Week Ten

Read chapters 10 and 12, "Pass the Healing On" and "Close Today, Closer Tomorrow."

1. In order to assess the healing God has been doing in you and your marriage, go back to chapter 5 and redo the inventory of your symptoms and problems on pages 71–72, evaluating the impact of your past on pages 75–76, and your view of sex on pages 77–78.

2. How have your answers to these inventories and surveys changed from when you first answered them?

3. What would you still like God to change or heal in you?

4. What changes have you seen in your marriage? in your husband? Ask your husband to describe the changes he's seen in you and your marriage. Write down what he says.

5. Redo the inventory of your marriage on pages 124–125. What would you like to see change and continue to heal in the three areas—spiritual, emotional, and physical—in your marriage?

6. Read Philippians 1:6. How does this verse give you hope that God will continue to work in you and your marriage?

7. How have you begun to see God use you in new ways as a parent, friend, and leader because of your healing?

8. What's the next step God is leading you to in your healing?

AN INVITATION

Congratulations! You've worked hard, and I'm proud of you. It took courage to take this journey, to trust God to heal your past and restore the lost intimacy in your marriage. Like many other courageous women before you, you've been brave enough to trust and strong enough to resist the urge to settle for "how it is" and reach for "what could be." You've been willing to step toward your future by surrendering your past.

God led you to this place and will walk with you to the end...never leaving you, never giving up on you. He'll never be frustrated with your needs or desires or how many tears you cry. He offers no judgment or condemnation, regardless of what your past holds. And He has no deadline for you to meet. Instead He's a God of gifts—limitless gifts of love, understanding, patience, and grace.

Since long before this book reached your hands, I've been praying for you. That God would prepare you with open ears to hear this message and with a softened heart to receive its truth. That you'd be willing to say yes to Him, to trust Him, and to follow as He leads you to greater intimacy with Himself and your husband.

And though I may not have the pleasure of meeting you and hearing your story, I'm confident that we'll be introduced in heaven one day, and then we'll have all eternity to share together the great things God has done.

Please visit me at my Web site, www.barbarawilson.org, where you can contact me with your comments and questions...and maybe share a bit of your story.

I'd love to hear from you.

Blessings,

Barbara

Acknowledgments

I'm overwhelmed with gratitude to those who have been a part of making this book possible.

To Multnomah for being willing to take a second chance on a new author and publish this book. For recognizing the heart and need of this message and having the courage to offer it to a hurting, wounded world very much in need of healing.

To David Kopp and Alice Crider: Thank you for championing this project to your publishing house and freely offering support, encouragement, and guidance throughout the process.

To Liz Heaney: You are amazing at what you do. I know it's a far better book because of your expert fingerprints embedded in every page. You challenged, stretched, and grew me as a writer. I'm grateful for how you've taken my humble offerings and formed them into the best book it can be.

To Rachel, who encouraged me to begin the sexual healing Bible study at Bayside Church in Granite Bay, California: Without you, there'd be no women finding healing and no stories for me to share—and no partner with whom to celebrate this ministry.

To the women who've shared their stories with me: Thank you for trusting me with your deepest secrets. Thank you for trusting God to heal your sexual wounds and for letting me encourage others through your journeys. This book is dedicated to all of you.

To my family, who love and support me: Thank you for being willing to share your daughter, wife, and mom with others. You'll be rewarded one day.

To my best friend, my husband: Thank you for devoting your life to encouraging me to reach for all that God has for me. You've given your life, as much as I have, to helping others find healing and hope. Their words of gratitude to me are meant for you as well.

And to the greatest love of my life, my Lord, heavenly Father, and dearest Friend: I continue to be astonished, amazed, and humbled that the King of the universe would want to know me, love me, and use me. Thank You for setting my heart free for You. Even more, thank You for choosing me to be Your voice of grace and healing to those who have yet to find their way. Because of You, I have a heart that can't stop singing.

Notes

Introduction

1. Robert Rector, "The Effectiveness of Abstinence Education Programs in Reducing Sexual Activity Among Youth," *The Heritage Foundation,* April 8, 2002, www.heritage.org/Research/Abstinence/BG1533.cfm.

Chapter 1: Saying No When You Want to Say Yes

1. Lawrence B. Finer, "Trends in Premarital Sex in the United States, 1954–2003," *Public Health Reports* 122 (January–February 2007): 73.

Chapter 2: The "Superglue" Hormone

1. I wrote about this in chapter 3 of my first book, *The Invisible Bond: How to Break Free from Your Sexual Past* (Multnomah, 2006). For the sake of clarity, I've adapted some of that material here. I've also added information from more recent research on the brain.

2. Joe S. McIlhaney, Jr. and Freda McKissic Bush, *Hooked: New Science on How Casual Sex Is Affecting Our Children* (Chicago: Northfield, 2008), 35.

3. Douglas Weiss, *The Final Freedom: Pioneering Sexual Addiction Recovery* (Fort Worth, TX: Discovery, 1998), 17–24.

4. Eric Keroack and John R. Diggs, Jr., "Abstinence Statistics and Studies: The Bonding Imperative," The Abstinence Clearinghouse, Dec. 31, 2002, www.abstinence.net.

5. Irina Bosse, "Oxytocin: A Hormone for Love," *Future Frame,* September 24, 1999, www.morgenwelt.de.

6. McIlhaney and Bush, *Hooked,* 45.

7. R. A. Turner, M. Altemus, T. Enos, B. Cooper, and T. McGuinnes, "Preliminary Research on Plasma Oxytocin in Normal Cycling Women:

Investigating Emotion and Interpersonal Distress" *Psychiatry* 62, no. 2 (Summer 1999), www.oxytocin.org/oxy/oxywomen.html.

8. Eric Keroack, *The Oxytocin Cell,* presented at the National Abstinence Clearinghouse Conference, Kansas City, June, 2006, www.slideshare.net/rhrc/the-oxytocin-cell.

9. Keroack and Diggs, "Abstinence Statistics and Studies: The Bonding Imperative," Dec. 31, 2002. The Abstinence Clearinghouse, www.abstinence.net.

10. Joan R. Kahn and Kathryn A. London, "Premarital Sex and the Risk of Divorce," *Journal of Marriage and the Family* 53, no. 4 (November 1991): 845–855.

11. Andrew M. Greeley, *Faithful Attraction: Discovering Intimacy, Love and Fidelity in American Marriage* (New York: Tor, 1991), 201.

Chapter 3: When Sex Doesn't Bring Pleasure

1. National Campaign to Prevent Teen Pregnancy, *Not Just Another Thing to Do: Teens Talk About Sex, Regret, and the Influence of Their Parents,* April 27, 2000, www.thenationalcampaign.org/resources/pdf/pubs/NotJust_FINAL.pdf.

2. Michael R. Pergamit, Lynn Huang, and Julie Lane, *Long-Term Impact of Adolescent Risky Behaviors and Family Environment,* paper submitted to the Office of the Assistant Secretary for Planning and Evaluation, U.S. Department of Health and Human Services, 2001.

3. Gordon Neufeld and Gabor Maté, *Hold On to Your Kids: Why Parents Need to Matter More Than Peers* (New York: Ballantine, 2005), 159.

4. Kerstin Uväs-Moberg interview, "Oxytocin: World's expert talks about this calming hormone," *Life Science Foundation,* lifesciencefoundation.org/cmoxytocin.html.

5. Rose C. Mantella, Regis R. Vollmer, Xia Li, and Janet A. Amico, "Female

Oxytocin-Deficient Mice Display Enhanced Anxiety-Related Behavior,"
Endocrinology 144, no. 6 (2003), www.endo.endojournals.org/cgi/content/
full/144/6/2291.

Chapter 4: Emotionally Divided

1. Laura Sessions Stepp, *Unhooked: How Young Women Pursue Sex, Delay Love and Lose at Both* (New York: Riverhead Books, 2007), 27.

2. Stepp, *Unhooked,* 255.

3. Stepp, *Unhooked,* 260.

4. P. Roger Hillerstrom and Karlyn Hillerstrom, *The Intimacy Cover-Up: Uncovering the Differences Between Love and Sex* (Grand Rapids, MI: Kregel, 2004), 29.

5. Hillerstrom and Hillerstrom, *The Intimacy Cover-Up,* 28–29.

6. Hillerstrom and Hillerstrom, *The Intimacy Cover-Up,* 32.

7. P. Roger Hillerstrom, phone interview by author, October 4, 2005.

8. Rick Warren, *The Purpose Driven Life* (Grand Rapids, MI: Zondervan, 2002), 247.

Chapter 5: Where Does It Hurt?

1. Used with the permission of Mindy Johnson, HEART director, Pregnancy Resource Centers of Greater Portland.

Chapter 6: A Plan for Healing

1. Rick Warren, *The Purpose Driven Life* (Grand Rapids, MI: Zondervan, 2002), 247.

2. Henry Cloud and John Townsend, *How People Grow* (Grand Rapids, MI: Zondervan, 2001), 206.

3. John Eldredge and Stasi Eldredge, *Captivating: Unveiling the Mystery of a Woman's Soul* (Nashville: Nelson, 2005), 59.

Chapter 7: Say Good-Bye to the Past

1. Eric Keroack, *The Oxytocin Cell,* presented at the National Abstinence Clearinghouse Conference, Kansas City, June, 2006, www.slideshare .net/rhrc/the-oxytocin-cell.
2. These steps are adapted from my first book, *The Invisible Bond.*
3. Prayer created by Kathy Edwards and used by permission.
4. Henry Cloud and John Townsend, *How People Grow* (Grand Rapids, MI: Zondervan, 2001), 172.

Chapter 8: Become Your Husband's Best Friend

1. David Ferguson, Teresa Ferguson, Chris Thurman, and Holly Thurman, *Intimate Encounters: A Practical Guide to Discovering the Secrets of a Really Great Marriage* (Nashville: Thomas Nelson, 1994), 1.
2. Alfred Ells, *Restoring Innocence: Healing the Memories and Hurts That Hinder Sexual Intimacy* (Nashville: Thomas Nelson, 1990), 161–162.
3. Ells, *Restoring Innocence,* 166–167.

Chapter 9: It's Time to Be Lovers Again

1. Linda Dillow and Lorraine Pintus, *Intimate Issues: 21 Questions Christian Women Ask About Sex* (Colorado Springs, CO: WaterBrook, 1999), 6–10.
2. Helen Fisher, quoted in Lauren Slater, "This Thing Called Love," *National Geographic,* February 2006, 48.

Chapter 11: Common Questions, Helpful Answers

1. Dr. Dan B. Allender, *The Wounded Heart: Hope for Adult Victims of Childhood Sexual Abuse* (Colorado Springs, CO: NavPress, 1990), 48.
2. Allender, *The Wounded Heart,* 48.

Bibliography

Alcorn, Randy, *Restoring Sexual Sanity.* Fort Lauderdale, FL: Coral Ridge
    Ministries, 2000.

Allender, Dan B., *The Wounded Heart: Hope for Adult Victims of Childhood
    Sexual Abuse.* Colorado Springs, CO: NavPress, 1990.

Cloud, Henry, and John Townsend, *How People Grow: What the Bible Reveals
    About Personal Growth.* Grand Rapids, MI: Zondervan, 2001.

Cochrane, Linda, *The Path to Sexual Healing.* Grand Rapids, MI: Baker,
    2000.

Conaway, Dr. Dale H., *Sex & the Bible.* Shippensburg, PA: Treasure House,
    1996.

Dillow, Joseph, Linda Dillow, Peter Pintus, and Lorraine Pintus, *Intimacy
    Ignited: Conversations Couple to Couple.* Colorado Springs, CO:
    NavPress, 2004.

Dillow, Linda, and Lorraine Pintus, *Intimate Issues: 21 Questions Christian
    Women Ask About Sex.* Colorado Springs, CO: WaterBrook, 1999.

Eden, Dawn, *The Thrill of the Chaste: Finding Fulfillment While Keeping Your
    Clothes On.* Nashville: W Publishing, 2006.

John Eldredge and Stasi Eldredge, *Captivating: Unveiling the Mystery of a
    Woman's Soul.* Nashville: Nelson, 2005.

Ells, Alfred, *Restoring Innocence: Healing the Memories and Hurts That Hinder
    Sexual Intimacy.* Nashville: Nelson, 1990.

Ethridge, Shannon, *Every Woman's Battle.* Colorado Springs, CO:
    WaterBrook, 2003.

Ferguson, David, Teresa Ferguson, Chris Thurman, and Holly Thurman,
    *Intimate Encounters: A Practical Guide to Discovering the Secrets of a
    Really Great Marriage.* Nashville: Thomas Nelson, 1994.

Greeley, Andrew M., *Faithful Attraction: Discovering Intimacy, Love and Fidelity in American Marriage.* New York: Tor, 1991.

Grossman, Miriam, M.D., *Unprotected.* New York: Penguin, 2006.

Hillerstrom, P. Roger, and Karlyn Hillerstrom, *The Intimacy Cover-Up: Uncovering the Differences Between Love and Sex.* Grand Rapids, MI: Kregel, 2004.

Joy, Donald, *Re-bonding: Preventing and Restoring Damaged Relationships,* 2nd ed. Napanee, IN: Evangel, 2000.

McIlhaney, Joe, S. Jr., and Freda McKissic Bush, *Hooked: New Science on How Casual Sex Is Affecting Our Children.* Chicago: Northfield, 2008.

Meeker, Meg, *Epidemic: How Teen Sex Is Killing Our Kids.* Washington, DC: LifeLine, 2002.

Neufeld, Gordon, and Gabor Maté, *Hold On to Your Kids: Why Parents Need to Matter More Than Peers.* NY: Ballantine, 2005.

Reisman, Judith A., *Kinsey: Crimes & Consequences.* Arlington, VA: Institute for Media Education, 2000.

Rinehart, Paula, *Strong Women, Soft Hearts,* Nashville, TN: W Publishing, 2001.

Rinehart, Paula, *Sex and the Soul of a Woman,* Grand Rapids, MI: Zondervan, 2004.

Smalley, Gary, *Making Love Last Forever.* Dallas: Word, 1996.

Stanton, Glenn T., *Why Marriage Matters: Reasons to Believe in Marriage in Postmodern Society.* Colorado Springs, CO: Pinon, 1997.

Stepp, Laura Sessions, *Unhooked: How Young Women Pursue Sex, Delay Love and Lose at Both.* New York: Riverhead, 2007.

Rick Warren, *The Purpose Driven Life,* Grand Rapids, MI: Zondervan, 2002.

Weiss, Douglas, *The Final Freedom: Pioneering Sexual Addiction Recovery.* Fort Worth, TX: Discovery, 1998.